AF208095

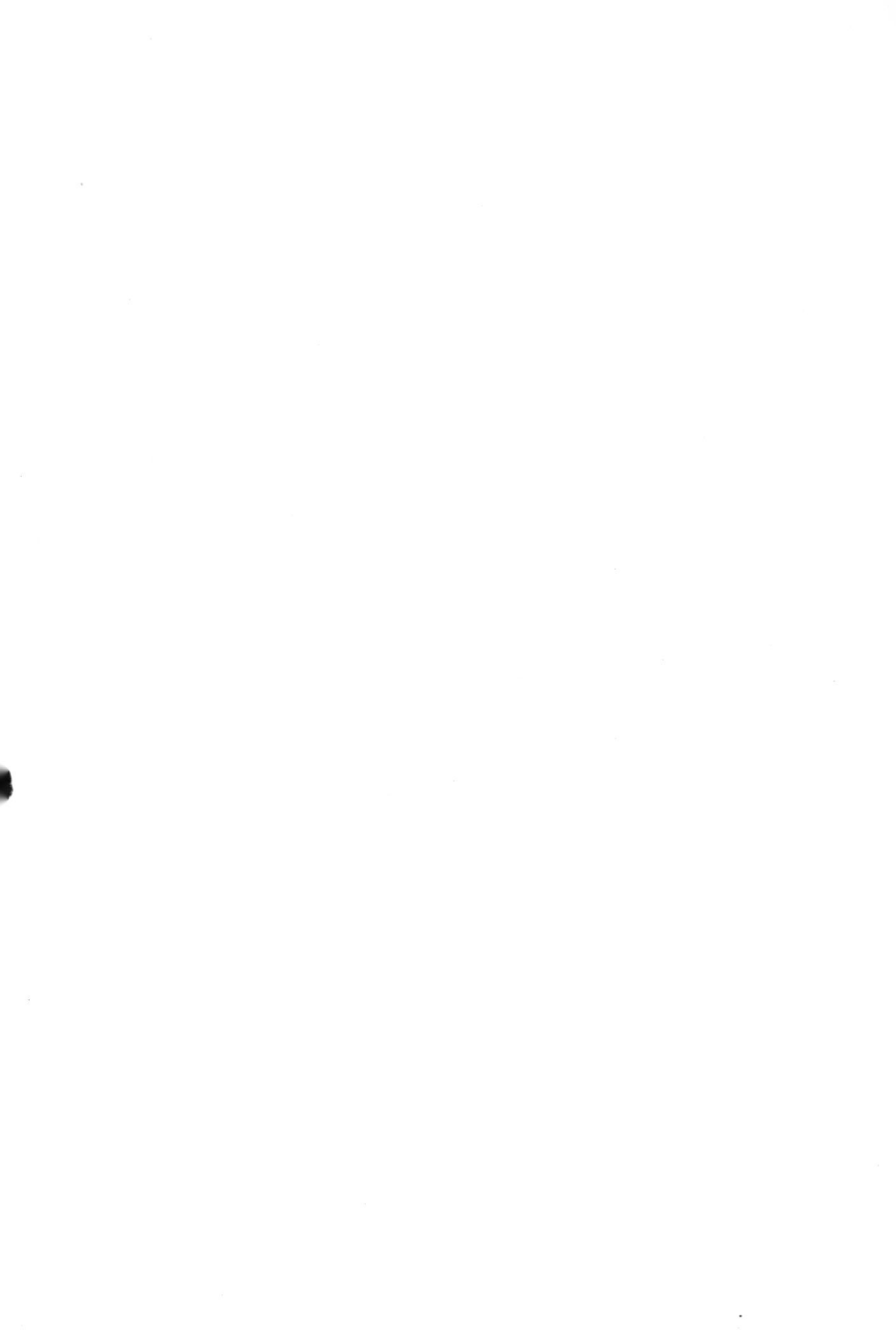

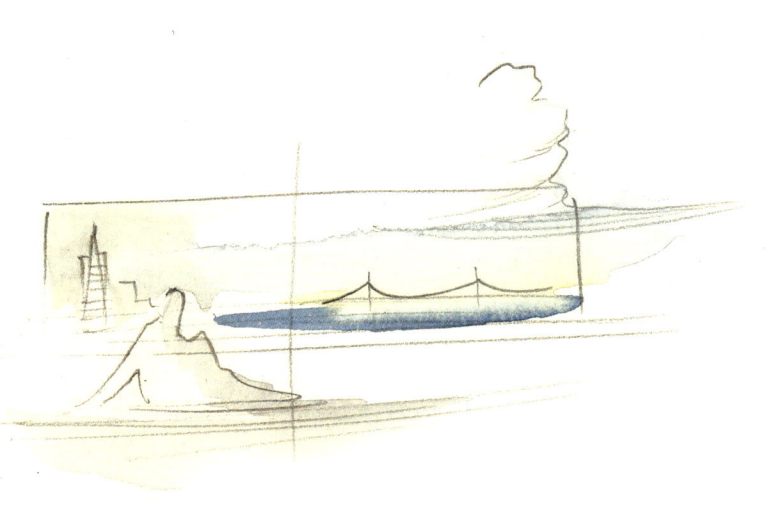

UNIVERSITY OF VIRGINIA PRESS

Charlottesville & London

Andrea Ponsi

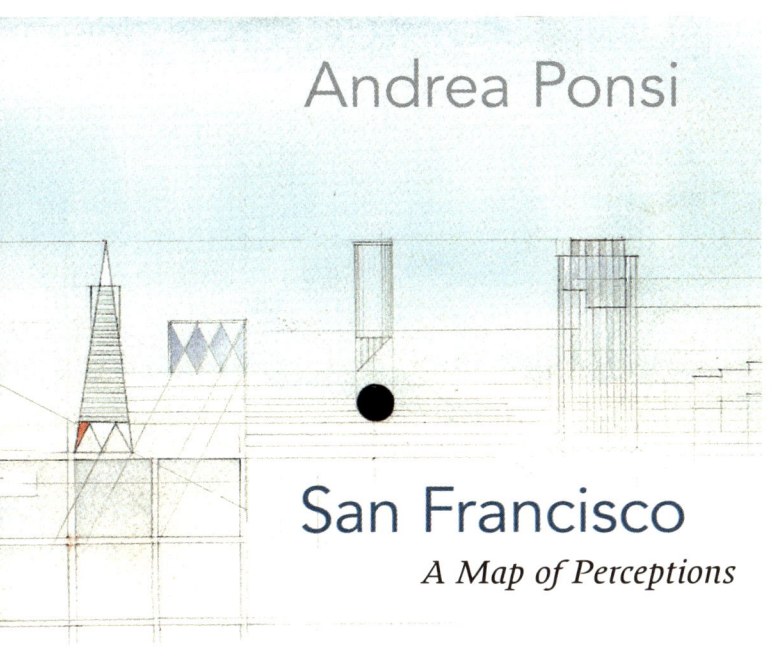

San Francisco

A Map of Perceptions

Translated by Susan Scott

University of Virginia Press
© 2015 by the Rector and Visitors of the University of Virginia
All rights reserved
Printed in China on acid-free paper
First published 2015

9 8 7 6 5 4 3 2 1

Library of Congress Cataloging-in-Publication Data
Ponsi, Andrea.
San Francisco : a map of perceptions / Andrea Ponsi ; translated
by Susan Scott.
     pages   cm
 ISBN 978-0-8139-3635-2 (cloth : alk. paper)
 1. Ponsi, Andrea—Themes, motives. 2. San Francisco (Calif.)—
In art. 3. San Francisco (Calif.)—Description and travel. I. Title.
 ND1962.P66A4 2014
 759.5—dc23

                                        2013050102

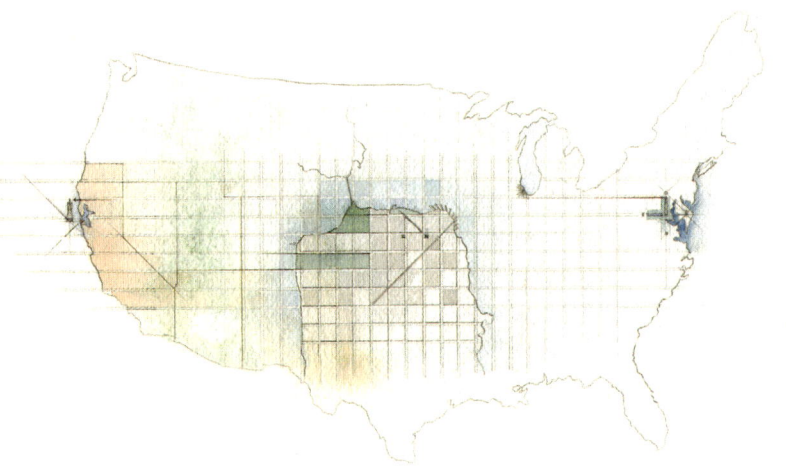

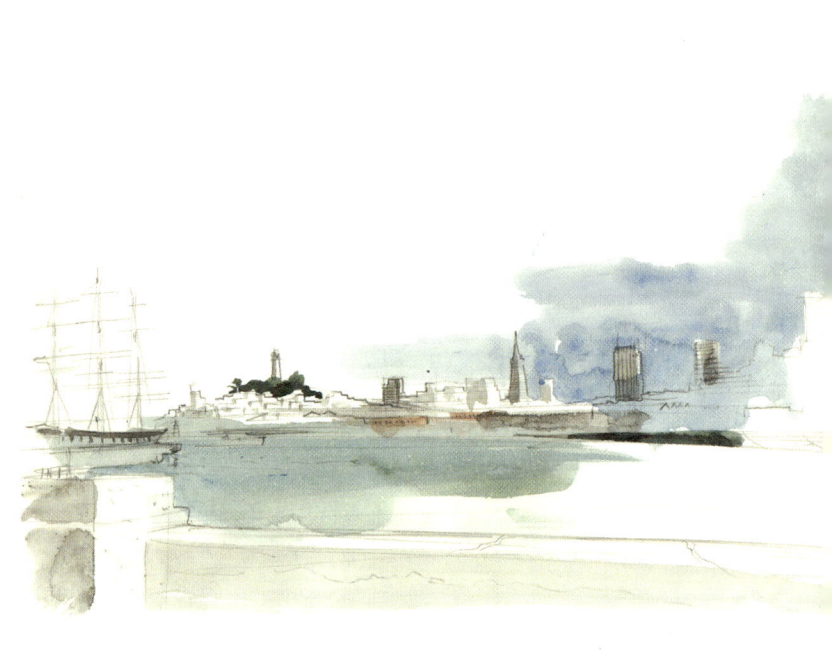

Arriving | Arriving in San Francisco from the north across the Golden Gate Bridge, *the first Indians.*

From the south, along the coast or the bay, on the freeways, *the missionaries and the campesinos from Latin America.*

From the east, across the Bay Bridge, *the whites from Europe and America.*

From the west, by sea or by air, *from China and Japan.*

Toponymy | There are no pelicans on Alcatraz, no angels on Angel Island, no treasures on Treasure Island, no oysters in Oyster Bay, no beaches at North Beach, no good grasses on Yerba Buena Island.

I Don't Live There Anymore | Thinking about San Francisco and writing the first words that come to mind: wind, light, bay, skyscrapers, bridge, Berkeley, Noe Valley, North Beach, rails, streetcar, bus, waiting for the bus at Mission Street, driving the freeways, exit, Washington Park, green lawns, sloping lawns, Dolores Park, Alcatraz, ships passing slowly by, ship horns in the night, fine drizzly rain, fog straddling the mountains, the cool breeze looking toward Angel Island, the bridge that looks like a necklace, the bridge that lights up at night, looking fearfully at the ocean, paying the toll, entering Lombard Street, climbing the hills, pressing on the gas pedal going uphill, entering South of Market, the lofts and warehouses, then downtown, the tops of the high-rises, thinking about the American city, the city where, at the end of the road, there is always a big bridge, roller coasters, Chinese gates, gleaming white marble department stores, going in one and wanting to come right out, finding myself in a square, hedges and jugglers, going into the parking lot, paying, coming out of the parking lot, crossing Chinatown, entering North Beach, the red wood of the Caffe Trieste, Columbus Avenue, the white spires of the church, Stockton Street, looking for my house, looking up, the door is closed, I don't know the names on the doorbells, I don't live there anymore; I haven't lived there for more than twenty years.

The House in North Beach | The house on Stockton Street, in North Beach, was a three-story building with six apartments, two on each floor. Like all the others on the street, the house had two faces: the façade on the street decorated and embellished; the one in back simple, stripped-down and functional, but maybe more beautiful.

From the street the house looked like a female body: the two breasts were the rounded bow windows; the

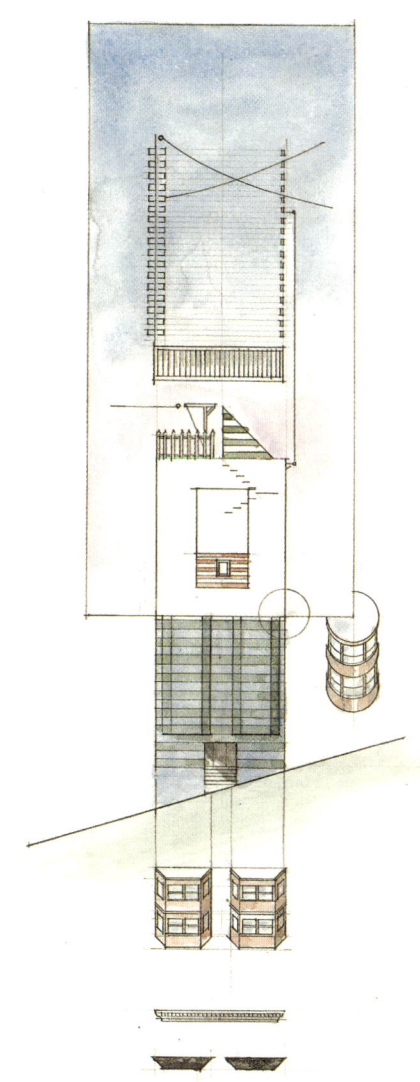

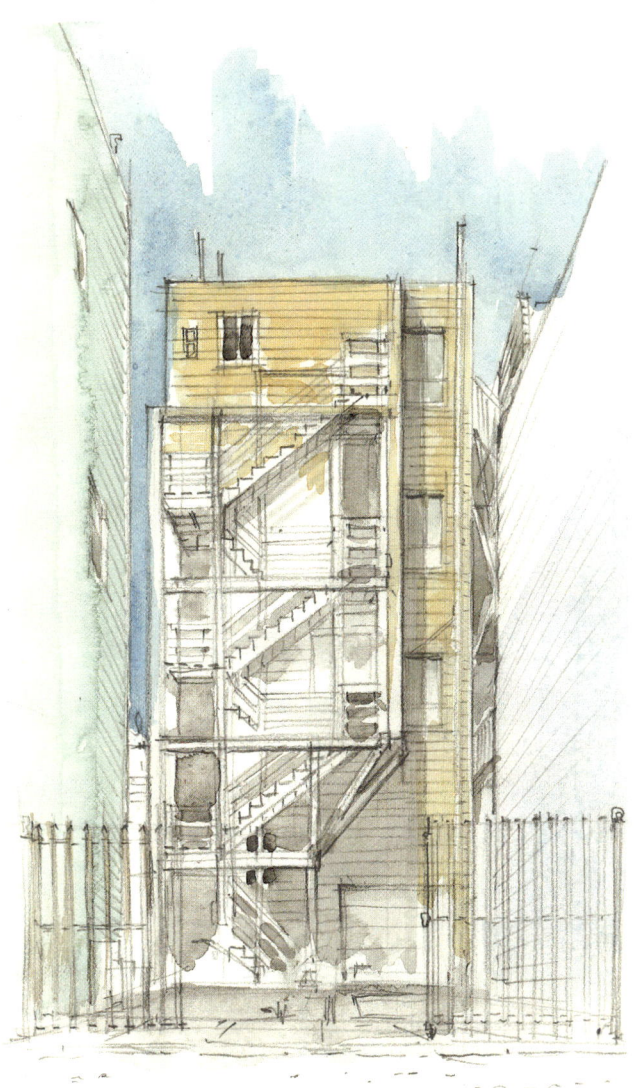

eyes, the double-hung windows; the eyelids, the roller blinds behind the glass; the eyelashes, the slightly affected Victorian dentil molding of the cornice under the eaves.

In back, it was a different house. Nothing was done for effect: just horizontal wooden boards, simply painted white. The outside stairs, also wooden, were intimate and safe, and the clotheslines stretched away from the windows to reach self-standing poles with pegs, totem sculptures, slender ladders to the sky.

But to discover the most sublime aspect of the house, you had only to climb the outside stairs up to the terrace: a wooden deck surrounded by a railing and resting on the roof. Here the universe opened up: the city spread out all around like a kasbah. The pink, white, and blue houses were a child's toy blocks. The bay stretched blue-green, dotted with sails and plowed by ships. Farther away, the islands, the promontories, the Golden Gate, and then the ocean.

The deck of the North Beach house was the bridge of a ship, the rooftop terrace of a palace in Zanzibar, a paradise room floating in midair.

Profile | A city by the sea whose whiteness shines brightest in the afternoon light. Then it turns golden when its highest, most massive building, fluted like a diamond, reflects the light of the setting sun. Then silvery, like the sky at dusk, which over the ocean is an intense red like the horizon in a Japanese print. When night falls, the city lights up with millions of lanterns, and downtown is transformed into a luminous ocean liner.

Houseboats | Houseboats, like the little ones floating in the shallow water of the bay at Sausalito; tidy and orderly as the houses in a subdivision, they are anarchic in their individual look. Well-established by now, they are nothing like the primitive houseboats of the hippies. Now they are equipped with all the comforts, cable TV and satellite dishes.

Beyond the bay can be seen the biggest houseboat of all, the city-boat of San Francisco: dozens of buildings, warehouses, piers, wooden houses lined up along uphill streets. When the tops of its high-rises barely stick up out of the fog enveloping them, the whole city seems to float on the waters of the bay.

Fog | How many kinds of fog are there in San Francisco? The rarefied, almost transparent fog that lets the blue of the sky through. Or the fog that, like a big blanket, settles over the islands and hills, turning them into secret white tumuli. There is the fog that, once it has sifted through the big bridge, unravels across the bay to graze against Alcatraz and Angel Island, still in the sun. And there is the intense, cold fog that wraps around us on the quiet streets of the Sunset or the Richmond, toward Ocean Beach. There, even daytime is a damp, gray night.

There are other fogs, dozens of other kinds, depending on the neighborhood, the time of day, the position of the sun: fog sliced by swords of light, fog that unrolls in vaporous puffs, fog that bleaches the colors of the ships on the bay or envelops the antennas of Twin Peaks like a bush enwraps a cactus in the desert.

San Francisco, city of fog: a fog of many faces, changeable, capricious, imposing.

Seagulls | I watch the seagulls flying over the bay. Some will alight next to the tables at Sam's Anchor Cafe in Tiburon, hoping to grab a tidbit or two of boiled crab. Others zoom past, just grazing the water on their way to join their buddies at Alcatraz, and still others fly high toward the mounts of Presidio or Twin Peaks. There are also the ones that stand still, solitary, contemplating the world from a pole stuck in the water, or flutter about with other gulls in the wake of a ship headed toward Oakland.

Like pigeons in a city square, the gulls make the bay

their own: a vast open space, rich with food, games, opportunities.

The Grid | Looking at a map of San Francisco, one notices that the city is divided into three main zones, corresponding to three different street patterns. The dominant one is a squared grid running north-south, which takes in all the central part of the city, adjacent to the bay and to Ocean Beach. This precise geometry is interrupted only by the irregular Presidio grounds and the sinuous roads running inside Golden Gate Park.

The second pattern results from the disruption of this grid by the diagonal cut of Market Street. The whole area South of Market consists of a 45-degree turn of this same grid. This shift remains in place all the way to South Van Ness, where the streets swivel once again to resume the north-south orientation of the city.

The third pattern is found around the heights of Twin Peaks. There the streets completely abandon the rules of the grid, their paths resembling a tangle of coiled hair.

Overlaid on these street patterns, but totally inde-pendent of them, are the freeways that, flouting all

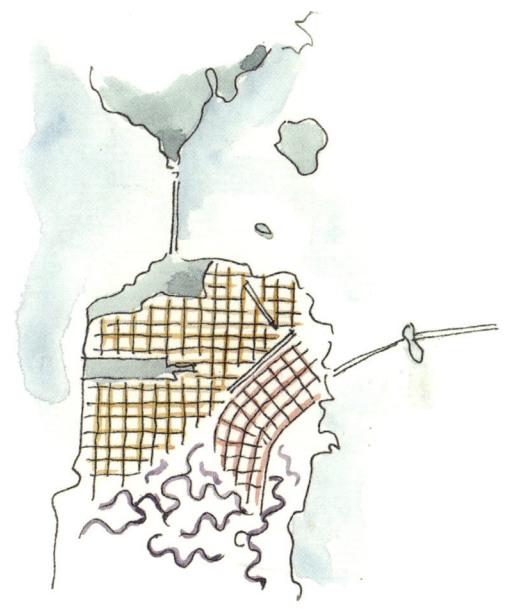

rules, stretch across the city like snakes slithering along the ground.

Dolores Street | Once I made drawings of San Francisco's streets, not from life, but as I remembered them. One of them was Dolores Street. It was a vertical drawing. In the lower part of the paper I outlined

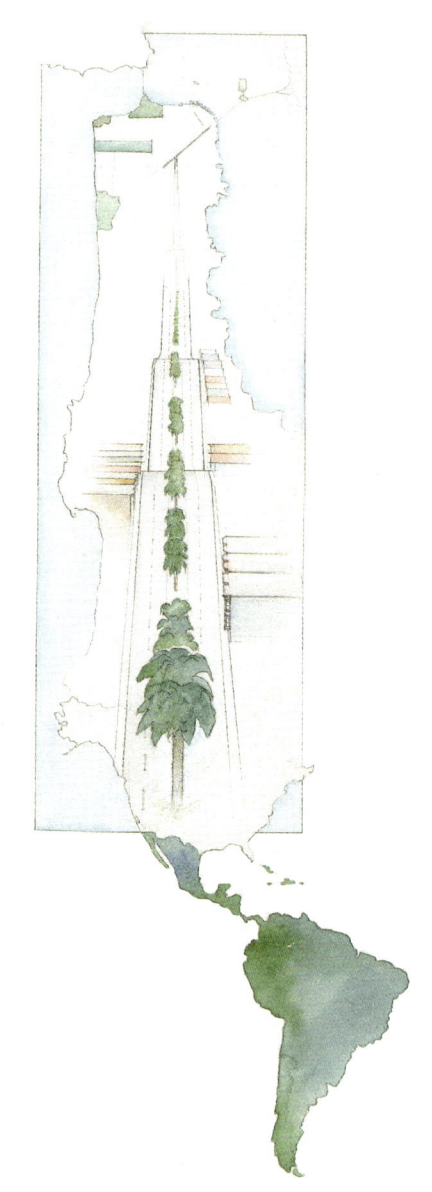

the precise profile of Latin America. Using watercolors I flooded it with green, as though the entire continent were one big tropical forest. Toward the top, after the Isthmus of Panama, the continent widened in the shape of Mexico, then mutated, with a highly imaginative leap of scale, into the layout of the San Francisco peninsula. There, the green mass became, in a rapid metamorphosis, a row of equally green tropical palm trees lined up in the middle of Dolores Street. The street then went on, in perspective, to flow into Market Street.

Dolores Street is the last segment of a path that over time has brought the people of Latin America to San Francisco. It is the symbol of this path and of its point of arrival: the point where the Mission District and the palm trees of Dolores Street merge with the American downtown.

Waters | Treacherous, cold, tormented are the waters of the ocean.

Energetic, cool, and ruffled the waters flowing through the Golden Gate.

Gray, still, marshy the waters of the rest of the bay.

The Interrupted Grid | The street grid made up of straight lines and right angles covers the entire city—sometimes it is oriented in a north-south direction, following the original grid of Yerba Buena, the little plot of urbanized ground that became San Francisco; other times it is on a slant relative to the older grid.

The plan to spread the grid like a blanket over the entire territory was not unopposed. Many, seeing the grid as a gift to real estate speculators whose purposes were suited by such an elementary form of urban planning, would have preferred a model more in keeping with the hilly configuration of the entire peninsula. Despite these criticisms, despite the attempts of architects in the City Beautiful movement to temper the cold geometry of the grid with a system of radiating boulevards, despite the few isolated examples of naturalistic landscaping carried out on the summits of some hills such as Telegraph Hill, the grid won the battle. Even now it reigns unchallenged, fighting only its own topographical incongruence, the city's steep climbs, its dangerous descents.

But the streets, straight as arrows, have not always succeeded in prevailing over the steeper hills. At times the grid breaks off, and the street, built for vehicular traffic, is forced to change into something else. This

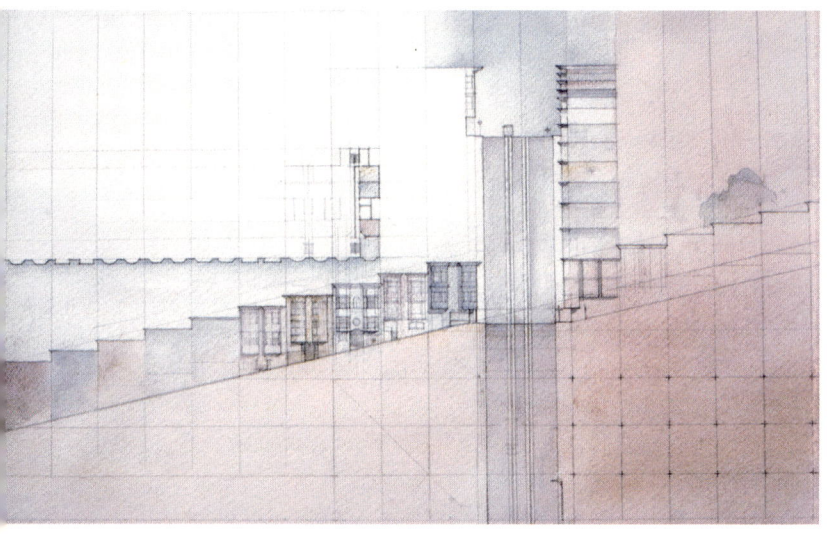

phenomenon of an interrupted street is expressed in
at least five ways. The first is its transformation into
a beautiful staircase, according to the circumstance
either rural in flavor, as on Filbert Street at Telegraph Hill, or Classical, as along Upper Lyon Street at
Vallejo Street. Next is the configuration of the street
as narrow, winding ramps, as in the famous Lombard Street. The third case totally gives up the idea of
ramps, stairs, or whatever, leaving a green space in the

shape of a practically vertical garden. And sometimes, when all attempts to solve the traffic thoroughfare problem are abandoned, the slope is simply filled up with houses and tall buildings so as to create a double superblock. Finally, the most radical solution: digging a tunnel under the hills, as was done in the 1930s on Stockton Street and then in the 1960s on Broadway. With the long-standing and long-debated problem solved at its root, motorists are able to pass from one part of the city to the other in a few quick seconds.

Entering | The most spectacular entrance into San Francisco is undoubtedly as you come out of the tunnel that, just after Sausalito, opens onto the Golden Gate Bridge and the city. After half a mile of darkness dug into the mountain, a semicircle of light perfectly frames the two pylons of the great bridge. Then the vision reveals itself in all its magnificent splendor, and the white city of San Francisco appears sparkling by the bay.

After a big downhill curve, the road comes onto the bridge. And while the car speeds through the red portals cut out of the pylons, on the left, beyond the steel cables that seem to hang from the sky, Alcatraz, Angel Island, and the East Bay Hills slide past; on the other side, the infinite vastness of the ocean.

20

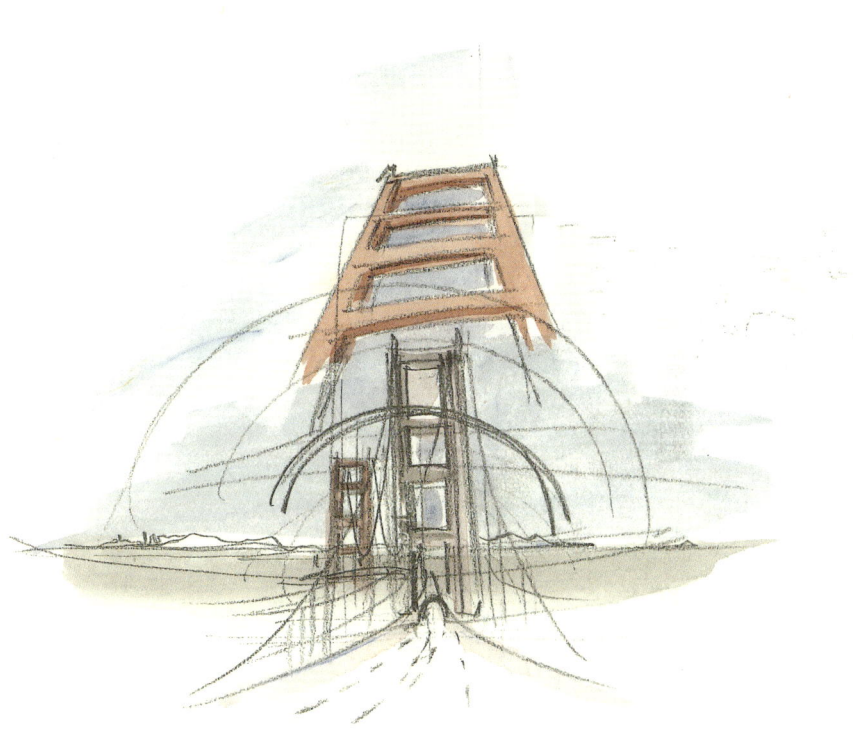

The Monument | Some big cities identify with a monument that surpasses all others through either its physical dominance or its symbolic importance. Rome has St. Peter's, Paris the Eiffel Tower, New York the Empire State Building. San Francisco has the Golden Gate Bridge. Nothing else in San Francisco threatens this dominion. The Golden Gate Bridge is San Francisco itself, its gate to the ocean, its crown, its red steel cathedral, its perfect image. San Francisco, too, is a bridge city, a gate, a cathedral glimpsed in the distance, a point of arrival, a beacon orienting those who have sought, are seeking, and perhaps will seek.

East-West | The Golden Gate Bridge is a Japanese ideogram, a Shinto red portal planted in the middle of the water. Analogously to the portals that in Japan face east, here the bridge faces west. It is a geographical oxymoron: Here, looking west, one goes to meet the East. There, looking east, one finds the West.

Pacific | I get into the car by the cliffs in Marin County overlooking the Pacific Ocean. It is a clear day, but the mist on the sea covers the line of the horizon. Outside the car, a cold wind is blowing. The Farallon Islands cannot be seen; only an indistinct light blur

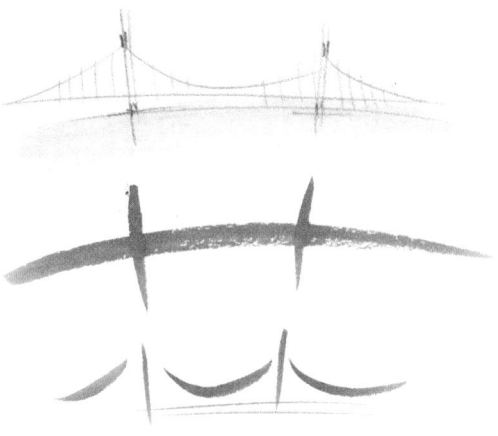

divides the leaden blue of the sea from the intense
azure of the sky.

The Pacific is an ocean that does not say where it
leads, that hides its destinations. An ocean that from
here seems to reject us or deceive us. Where are the
shipwrecked bodies of Gordon Pym or Captain Ahab?
Where are the numerous unlucky travelers who headed
to the happy isles of the South Seas? Down there,
beyond the fog, the treasures of Poe, Stevenson, or
Melville may exist. From here, the ocean appears only
as an indistinct abyss suggestive of macabre adven-
ture, a plausible image of what death may be.

I Wish | I wish I didn't have to talk about the hundreds of men and women who have killed themselves by jumping off the Golden Gate Bridge. I wish I didn't have to think about the car that I saw a little while ago stopped on the roadway while others drove slowly past it on either side; maybe someone got out of that car and jumped over the railing. I would like not to say that at least thirty people every year commit suicide here, three people every month, maybe one today, the one who got out of the car stopped on the roadway a little while ago. I wish it were not true.

The San Francisco Art Institute | I have almost reached the Chestnut Street entrance of the San Francisco Art Institute, a building made of exposed reinforced concrete and yet very traditional in architectural style. From outside it looks like a little church in an Italian village, complete with a bell tower in the Romanesque style. A stylistic oxymoron, Romanesque-Concrete.

After entering through the New Mannerist portal, I find myself in an open-air atrium, a bit Arabic because of the central fountain with colored ceramic tiles, a bit Italian monastery, a bit Mexican-Hispanic in flavor. A calm, meditative space, well-proportioned, where the splashing of the fountain merges with the cawing of crows in nearby trees.

Abandoning myself to the circular logic of monasteries, I walk along one of the galleries leading away from the entrance cloister. Hanging rather haphazardly on the walls is the students' artwork, for the most part paintings on wood or paper. I keep going straight, putting off until later entering the gallery with a fresco by Diego Rivera, beyond a door on my left. A few steps more and here is the magnificent surprise: a large open-air terrace, enclosed on three sides, with the fourth framing a sweeping view of the bay. The contrast is beautiful and violent; the only element shared by the Romanesque-Hispanic cloister and this open space designed by the architect Paffard Keatinge-Clay in the 1960s is the material used, reinforced concrete. In Keatinge-Clay's wing, the concrete is perfectly consistent with the Modernist-Brutalist architecture and is treated with a mastery and sober elegance superior even to the legendary "play of magnificent forms in light" that characterize the works of the Swiss architect Le Corbusier, who was Keatinge-Clay's teacher and employer.

Four truncated conical skylights occupy the central space of the plaza. Functional monuments, sculptures

25

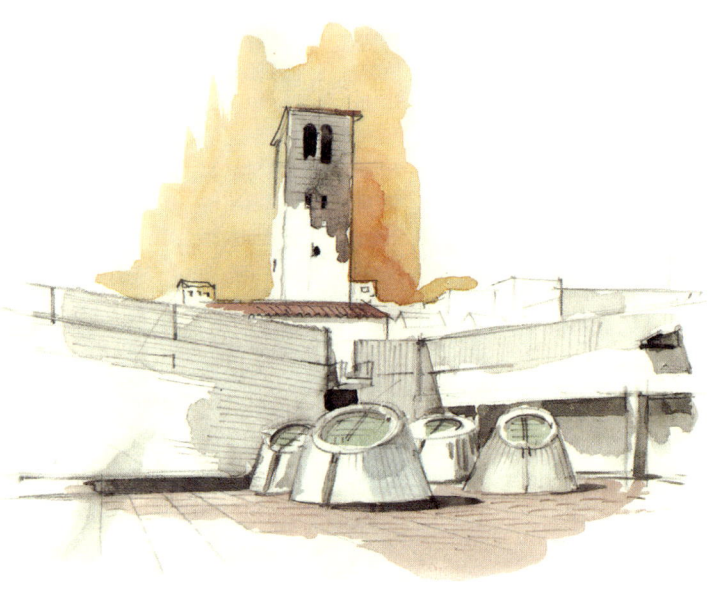

of light that channel the light into the studio space underneath.

I climb some stairs to the upper terrace. "Promenade architecturel," Le Corbusier would have called it, because of the sculptural forms of the auditorium and cafeteria and their masterful dialogue with the surrounding landscape. The broad, sloped roof of the auditorium is another open-air terrace, an ideal place to find peace, silence, and inspiration: all around is a panoramic view of the blue stretch of bay, Alcatraz, downtown San Francisco, and, in the distance, the East Bay Hills. Here the architect has been able to interpret perfectly the spirit of the already-existing "monastery school," developing the Neo-Romanesque complex in a light but powerful, absolutely Modern piece of architecture. All this without stylistic or mimetic compromise, but working by analogy with the spirit of Classical monasteries, their play of light and shade, the rhythm of the sequence of the space, the monumental elements that emerge.

San Francisco Lawns | The grass in San Francisco is not just green, it is deep green. It always looks fresh-cut. It is not even deep green: it is so bright that it is almost yellow, a transparent yellow, as if the sun had penetrated it and made it shine like a reflective surface. Is it that the grass is green or that the light is clear? So clear that it seems as if there is no air, no atmosphere, to blunt its force. Or is the sky so blue that it makes everything look more vivid, the grass greener, the houses whiter, the sun more yellow?

Fort Mason | The piers of Fort Mason stretch into the bay like the fingers on a hand. From here, in the 1940s, soldiers set out to fight in the Pacific. The Fort Mason piers float in the water like warships ready to

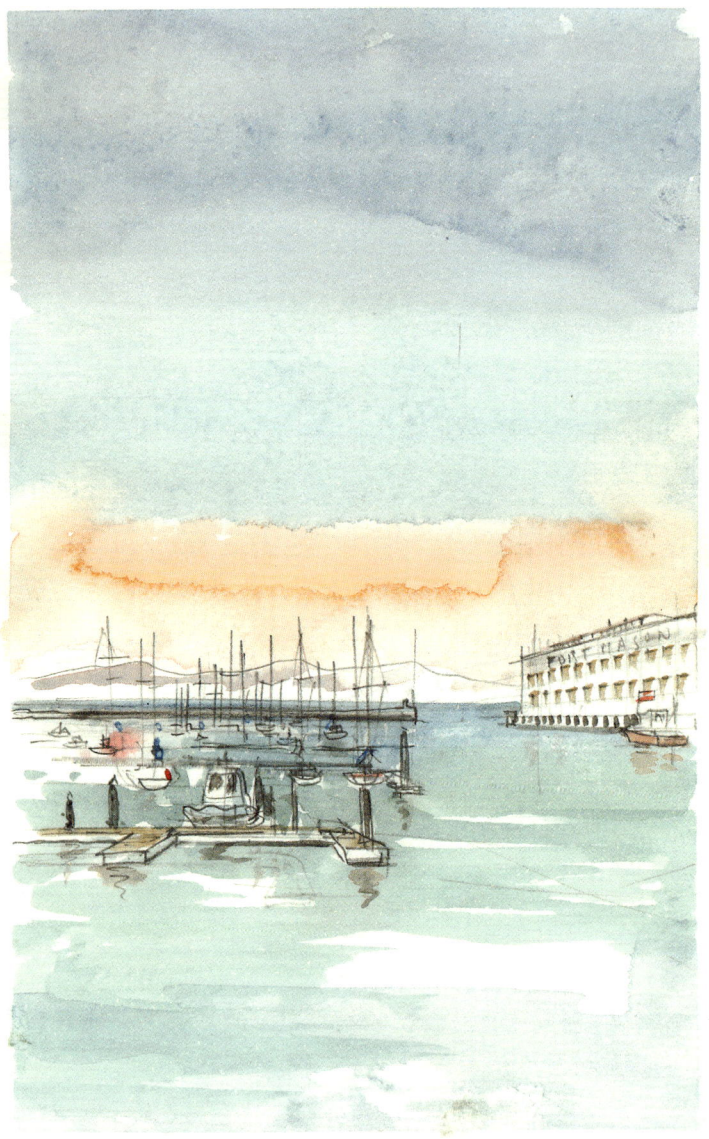

depart for adventurous expeditions, for futile wars, for unknown destinations. Happily, the piers stay in place. There are no longer soldiers and their commanding officers in the cabins or bombs and ammunition in the storehouses. Instead, the piers host organic restaurants, artists' studios, art galleries, workshops, schools of dance and tai chi.

Lombard Street | A mountain road, the steepest you can imagine, with hairpin curves within the space of a single block: the most tortuous street in the world is a sinuous serpent that uncoils along a garden slope to surprising effect. Seen from below, from Leavenworth Street, you cannot even see the pavement of the street. All that is visible is thick, low vegetation, a carpet of colorful hydrangeas incongruously traversed by the tops of automobiles slowly braving the climb.

Naturally, the street is one-way, and, distinguishing itself even further from all the other streets in San Francisco, it is paved with red bricks. Lombard Street provides an ingenious example of how to utilize a very steep slope that would otherwise require a pedestrian passageway with ramps and steps, as in the adjacent Filbert Street.

We talk about garden cities, garden neighborhoods, garden plazas. Lombard is certainly the most renowned garden street in the world. If you really think about it, a winding course like this could work even if the ground were flat. It would slow down the traffic and, just as on Lombard Street, create big yards in front of every house in the loop between one curve and the next. An unprecedented kind of street: the "winding garden street," even if perfectly flat.

Bar Mario | In the exact spot where I am now sitting, at Mario's Bohemian Cigar Store Cafe in North Beach, there used to be a pinball machine. Out of fashion and unprofitable, it was replaced by a table and chairs. A shame: I remember playing on it often, holding my little boy up, his tiny hands on the buttons to shoot the balls. But in everything else, Mario's is the same. A nice place, well-lit, right on the corner of the Victorian building that faces onto Washington Square Park. But since Columbus Avenue cuts through the square diagonally, and Mario's is right in the acute angle formed by Columbus, Mario's is a cutoff bar, a pointed bar, a polygon with three straight sides and one crooked one. It's better this way: more dynamic. Even without the pinball machine, it is still dynamic with people, and all the livelier because the many photos of that earlier time still hang on the walls. They didn't have to be moved to make space for another table.

Aquatic Park | I went back to Aquatic Park after long years away. I wanted to sit, like so many years ago, on those steps that make this place a little stadium, a calm, relaxing, open-air theater. I expected to find there, as I had every Saturday morning, people playing bongo drums, sunbathing, looking at the beach in front and the sailboats on the bay.

A metal fence with colored plastic tape blocks the entrance: "Construction Site." The steps of the bleachers have been torn up, waiting to be replaced or repaired with new concrete. The place looks like a

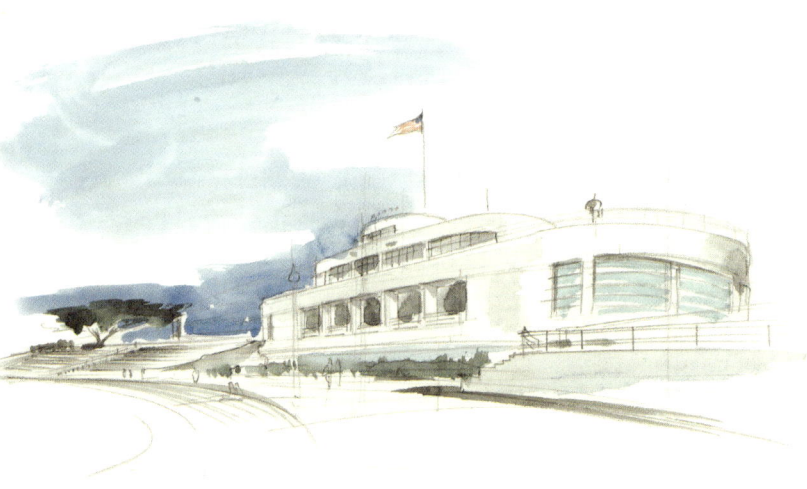

closed archaeological dig. Gone are the sounds of guitars and tambourines, the reggae beat seasoned with the smells of exotic herbs floating on the air. Aquatic Park, for another few weeks, or months, will just be torn-up bleachers, deserted, surrounded by a metal fence, cold and silent.

Washington Square Park | Washington Square Park is a perfect square, a green lawn with three trees in the middle. The square is interrupted along one side, in a peremptory, unapologetic gesture, by Columbus Avenue, which cuts through it diagonally: Columbus Avenue, a neighborhood diagonal, like Market Street, a city diagonal.

Washington Square Park is a synthesis of an Italian piazza and an English park. Slightly sloping to follow the gentle incline of the valley that was already there, it invites you to lie down on the grass, to stop for a cappuccino at one of the cafés along its edge, or to sit on a bench along the paved circle that runs around the grassy lawn, a circle that serves as a footpath, but is also useful for the police car on patrol. His arm leaning out the window, a policeman drives slowly by, checking out the territory: the bodies stretched out on the grass, the older people chatting, the homeless man squinting in the sunlight, the Chinese practicing tai chi.

Intersection | Three banks and three restaurants: this is the distribution of the six corners of the buildings at the intersection of Stockton and Union Streets, right where Columbus Avenue cuts through diagonally. The convergence of streets makes a nice intersection, dynamic, dense with people, a sort of flower with six petals of streets, six low, wedge-shaped buildings, each one on a corner, so many white lines on the ground, so many wires hanging in midair. The intersection is the realm of crosswalks, traffic lights, signs, streetcar cables, light poles.

3' x 3' | I am in North Beach, but like almost anywhere in San Francisco and perhaps in America, the sidewalks are made of concrete and are invariably divided by expansion seams into 3' × 3' squares. Except for this strict geometry, the concrete squares are always a little different. Sometimes they are scattered with dark stains of trampled chewing gum, sometimes dominated by cast-iron manhole covers. Some squares are interrupted by the red stripes of street curbs, others grooved by cracks in every direction. Some are dark gray from a certain mix of sand and cement, others almost white. Often they are damp and have a greenish tinge from lichens and mold, but other times they are perfect, freshly made. In any case,

33

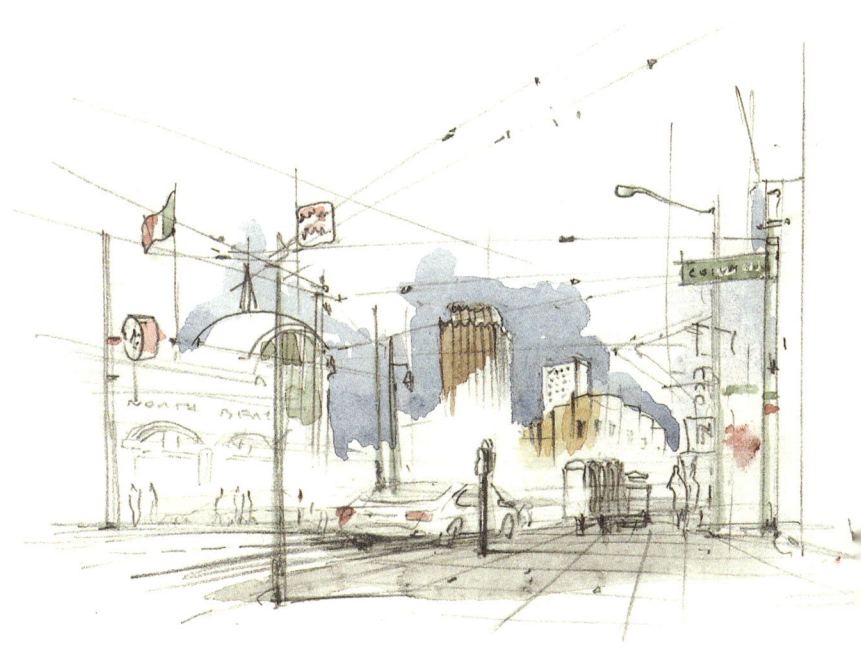

the 3' × 3' square is useful for setting the pace as you walk. To avoid stepping on the cracks, you have to take long steps, the steps of a person in good shape. Children need to take two steps to cross a square, the elderly one and one-half, a person walking slowly one and three-quarters.

Telegraph Hill | Once upon a time it was the hill with the telegraph. Now, in place of the telegraph, there is a tower, a monument that looks like a lighthouse, a Doric column, some say the nozzle of a fire hose. It seems that Mrs. Coit, who donated the tower, was crazy about firemen.

In any case, it is a simple, beautiful tower, an Art Deco version of a Classical pillar, fluted all the way up.

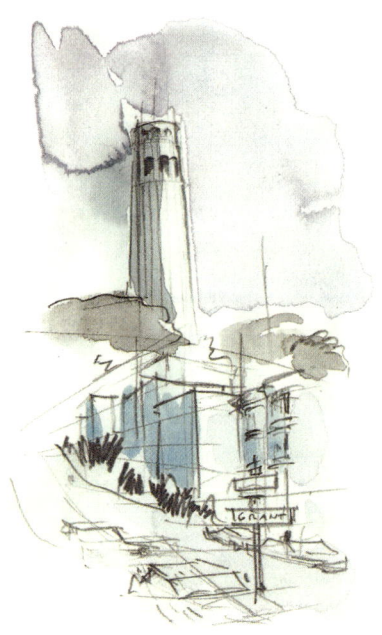

Certainly something purely artistic was needed on that hill to differentiate it from the overly functional towers downtown. Coit Tower stands there, the beacon on the telegraph island, protecting the little cubical houses perched all around the hill like a doting mother protects her young.

Street | What a strange effect these Victorian-style houses create, more or less all the same, two or at most three stories high, squeezed in one next to the other—they seem to be poised and trying to keep their balance on the too-steep street. The houses: consistent with gravity, sedate, well-mannered, nicely dressed, vertical. The street: transgressive, uneven, with no geometric rule, somewhat dangerous, almost impudent.

Caffe Trieste | I am sitting at a table at the Caffe Trieste. From this viewpoint, my eye embraces beyond the windows a fragment of the city: a sun-beaten yellow house, the outline of roofs on Grant Avenue, flat roofs sprinkled with chimneys, ladders, dentilated cornices; farther away, an American flag against a sky that is the brightest possible blue. On the glass are the letters ƎTƧƎIЯT ƎꟻꟻAꓛ, the mirror image of what the people passing on Grant Avenue read there. Under the lettering, customers sitting at the tables, cappuc-

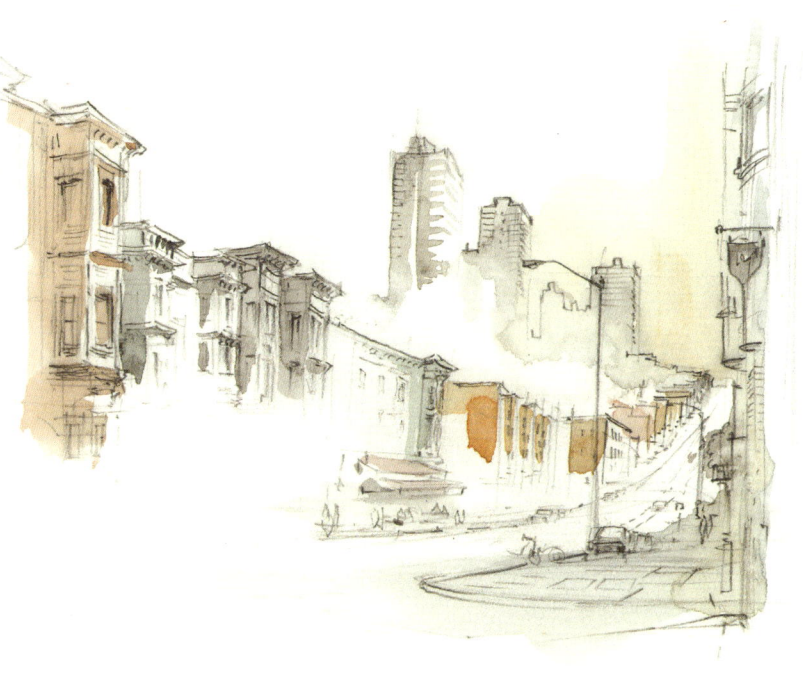

cinos, cups, empty chairs, rumpled newspapers, and an
old telephone booth (without a telephone); then more
chairs, other customers, maybe writers, ex-hippies, and
young, nameless wanderers. By now Bob Kaufman
doesn't come here anymore, his head in the clouds, or
Corso to read the newspaper. Maybe Jack Hirschman
still comes in to discuss socialism, and Ferlinghetti

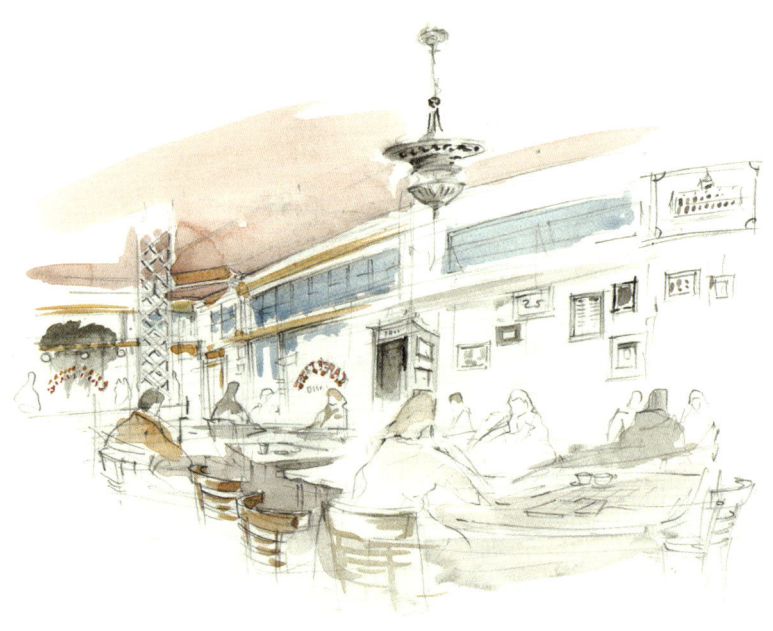

with a smile on his lips. I continue my inspection:
the table right in front of me has an imitation marble
top. On the tabletop is a sheet from the *San Francisco
Chronicle.* Then the sugar dispenser shaped like a glass
column, a cup with the marks of coffee, the open white
notebook, my hand holding the pen, and a tangled line
describing what it sees.

Thanks, Wall | This sounds banal, but hearing the piano being played nearby makes me think: this wall that separates the café interior from the street holds the sound, wraps it round and keeps it only for us. All for us this good jazz, this nice, gentle warmth (it's freezing outside); only for us this smell of coffee, this murmuring, these friendly glances, the voices . . .

City Lights Booksellers & Publishers

1   I approach the temple (of literature): City Lights Booksellers & Publishers. I am still on the other side of the street. The temple is there, a horizontal building, with a long black-and-yellow front window, running downhill on Columbus Avenue. You have to be alert crossing this multiple intersection: "No U-turn," "Freeway," "Broadway," "Stop," green, yellow, red lights. I am right on the ridge of a little hill, a minimal watershed between North Beach and Chinatown. The light is green; I cross.

Do I go in or look in the window first? Will Ferlinghetti still be there, upstairs, in his office? The books in the window speak of Zen, Ginsberg, Samuel Johnson, Jack Hirschman, Zapata, Duke Ellington. A hundred book covers arranged on a vertical wooden shelf cre-

ate a store window/shield, a veritable wall of defense
against the vulgarity besieging it from outside.

2   I cross the sacred threshold. The first thing I no-
tice, I hear. A soft music, jazz bordering on blues. I sit
right down on an isolated chair in the middle of the
shelves, a newer chair than those I remember from the
long-ago 1980s, when I used to come here. Hanging
on the wall is a street sign with the name in Italian:
"via [*sic!*] Ferlinghetti." I don't know if this street
exists, but the sign is here, ready. Right next to City
Lights is Kerouac Alley, a real street.

What should I do? Should I look at books or just
walk through the rooms and breathe the air of these
human papers? Breathe.

I go upstairs. A sign with an arrow points me
to "Poetry—Beat Generation." Another says, "San
Francisco Left Coast." And another one, "Books not
bombs." I sit down and think. If books were bricks,
one could create an architecture of beauty, freedom,
ideas, poetry. But books are bricks! Which people use
to build their identity, to construct the rooms of their
life, to create bridges, doors, windows. To be sure,
not all bricks are good or durable, but that is another
story.

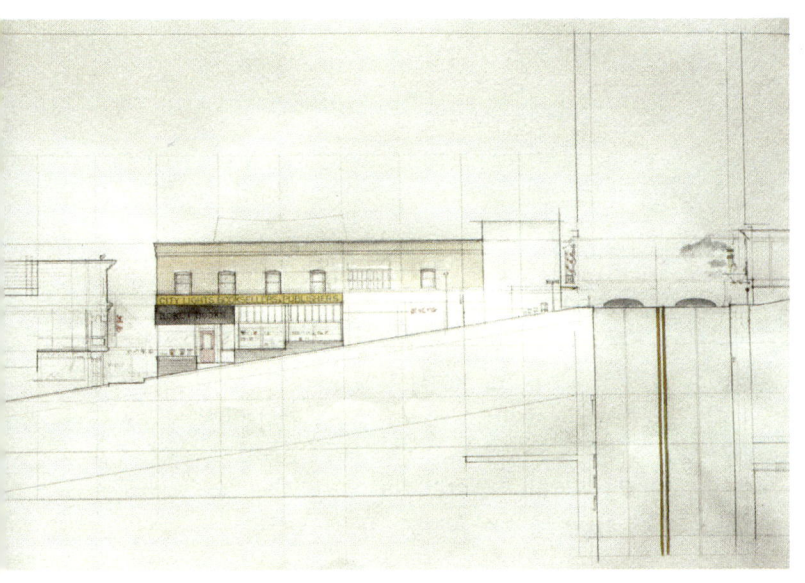

I climb up into the hermitage and sit down in what
a nearby sign identifies as the "poet's chair." It is
a rocking chair, right next to a window (but where
is Ferlinghetti?). On my left are shelves filled with
books; on my right is a window. Beyond the glass, on
a brick wall, I see a rusty fire escape, then the skyline
of downtown San Francisco no more than a half mile
away. The street noise comes in: the swish of buses,

Chinese voices. I rock in the poet's chair. If Ferlinghetti came by, what would I do? Say hello? Ask a
question? Or would I stay there, quietly reading something? This is a nice spot, this poet's chair next to the
window, the voices from the street, the books nearby.

3   The writer Ferlinghetti created City Lights, a
sanctuary of literature. The architect William Stout
has created a similar sanctuary: a bookstore devoted
to architecture. The two places are just a few blocks
from each other. The minds, the aspirations of these
two artist-booksellers are similar. The expressions,
the images, the rhythms hidden inside the respective
books in the two bookstores are similar.

As in a mirror, architecture and literature look at
one another, each recognizing in the other the ways
they are different and the ways they are similar. For
both, emotion, structure, the memory of the past, the
courage of the present, and vision are important. Each
one seeks something that belongs primarily to the
other: the architecture of the story, the story of the
architecture.

4   With every rock back and forth in the poet's (rocking) chair, the body recharges itself with poetry, like a

little clock, a spring-wound toy, gulps of oxygen for a deep-sea diver.

A city can evoke an emotion in us, inspire a sense of poetry. But even a simple chair, it seems, can do the same. Try it yourself. Come to San Francisco, go into City Lights, up to the second floor, and sit in the poet's chair. What do you feel? What comes to you that you absolutely have to say? What must you not say? Try it. All you have to do is rock, without saying anything, without writing.

5   I told myself I was going to describe the city using only words. No drawings or photographs. But what is the city? It is its spaces, intimate and infinite, unique and repeated a thousand times. It is its time, the time that lasts a second and the time that you can never say is over. It is its memory and the memory of the person living it. The past and the present moment. The city is its smells, sounds, noises, its forbidden things, its sins, duties, opportunities. Since it is all this and still more, I have tried to select some viewpoints from which to focus my gaze: the boundaries remain vague, but some words can help define it: sensations, space, architecture, material, paths, memory, relationships, imagination.

6   When Ferlinghetti dies, the Beat Generation will
be gone. From the poet's chair I see a photo with
Corso's impudent face, another with Kerouac and Neal
Cassady. I think about Allen Ginsberg, Gary Sny-
der, Bob Kaufman. With Lawrence Ferlinghetti's last
breath, San Francisco will become a different city.

Lamppost | This pole on the corner of a sidewalk
at the intersection of two streets is not just a lamp-
post. It is a tree. Its metal trunk grows more slender as
it rises. The first branches of steel are low. One holds
the pedestrian stoplight; inside its screen, dozens of
little red LEDs design an open hand, which then turns
white, indicating that it is safe to cross. Higher up,
another branch holds the street sign ("Grant Ave."),
then another, almost vertical, holds a bigger stoplight,
the traditional three-color traffic light. Another sign,
two feet up, says "No turns," then the sign for the cross
street ("California St.") and two arms from which
hang advertising banners. Finally, a very long arm, the
most important branch, juts out to the middle of the
intersection. A street lamp hangs from its point.
    The tree I have just described is fairly simple. It
doesn't have branches with the electric cables for the
buses, or the branches that at other intersections
support multiple traffic lights. But it is still a tree, an

evergreen. An urban tree, changeable not so much with the season as every single minute, the green, red, and yellow lights turning on and off. A tree useful for providing information, for keeping safe, to avoid getting run over, and decidedly local: as an icon, this one is very American and can be found everywhere, from the Atlantic to the Pacific.

P.S. | On Grant Avenue, Chinatown, these urban techno-trees take on a more ethnic look. Here they are painted light green, like jade, and even though they are completely similar to the others, a golden dragon wraps its tail around the pole, and its four legs hold a red lantern in the shape of a pagoda.

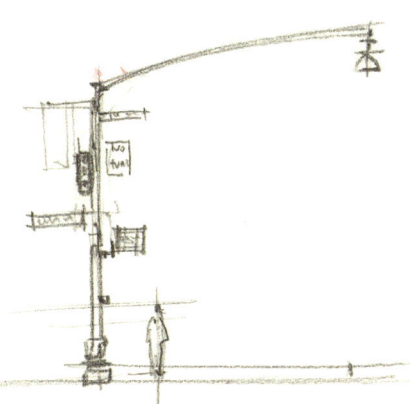

Beat Museum | *The Russians may have their Sputnik, but we have our beatniks here in North Beach.*
—Herb Caen, the *San Francisco Chronicle* reporter, after talking with Bob Kaufman, who had just finished reciting his Beat poems, accompanying himself on the bongo drum, on Adler Alley, right next to City Lights bookstore

A sign at the entrance to the Beat Museum explains the origin of the word "Beat." The Beat Museum is a strange combination of store, bookshop, and street museum that opened a few years ago on Broadway, in North Beach.

I enter warily, seeing all those T-shirts hanging on the wall and the gadgets on the counter. I'll be back out again in a minute, undoubtedly with a bad taste in my mouth, I tell myself. After browsing among historic photos and posters, copies of manuscripts, relics and memoirs, I start watching a film in which Ginsberg is reciting from Kerouac's *Dharma Bums.* I stand there, as though hypnotized, maybe an hour, maybe two, maybe ten, listening to that sublime voice reading one of the most poetic texts ever written.

Grant Avenue | In the length of a single block on Grant Avenue, the Italian American neighborhood becomes Chinatown. It is as though a river has suddenly changed the color of its water. Here, the cars rushing past on Columbus, banks, cafés, the bell tower, the Madonna over the portal of the church. There, past the traffic light, incomprehensible signs, the smell of wonton, red and green houses, dragons, the great Tao.

Chinatown | It is Saturday afternoon. I am sitting on a bench in a park full of Chinese. The park, a little plateau suspended on the boundary line between Chinatown and downtown, is a stage whose backdrop is a great wall of skyscrapers now lit by the setting sun.

Hundreds of people huddle together in little groups. The middle of the square is empty, just someone crossing it to get from one huddle to another. Inside the huddles, two kinds of games are being played: cards, laid on a makeshift piece of cardboard, or a type of checkers. Only two people play, but the entire group participates with shouts, orders, advice. I don't understand a thing. All these voices rise up in the park in sudden roars like flocks of pigeons taking flight. Foreign voices? But they've been living here for almost two hundred years! A foreign park? Why, it's in the middle of the city! Foreign faces? By now, in San Francisco, there is no face that you can call foreign.

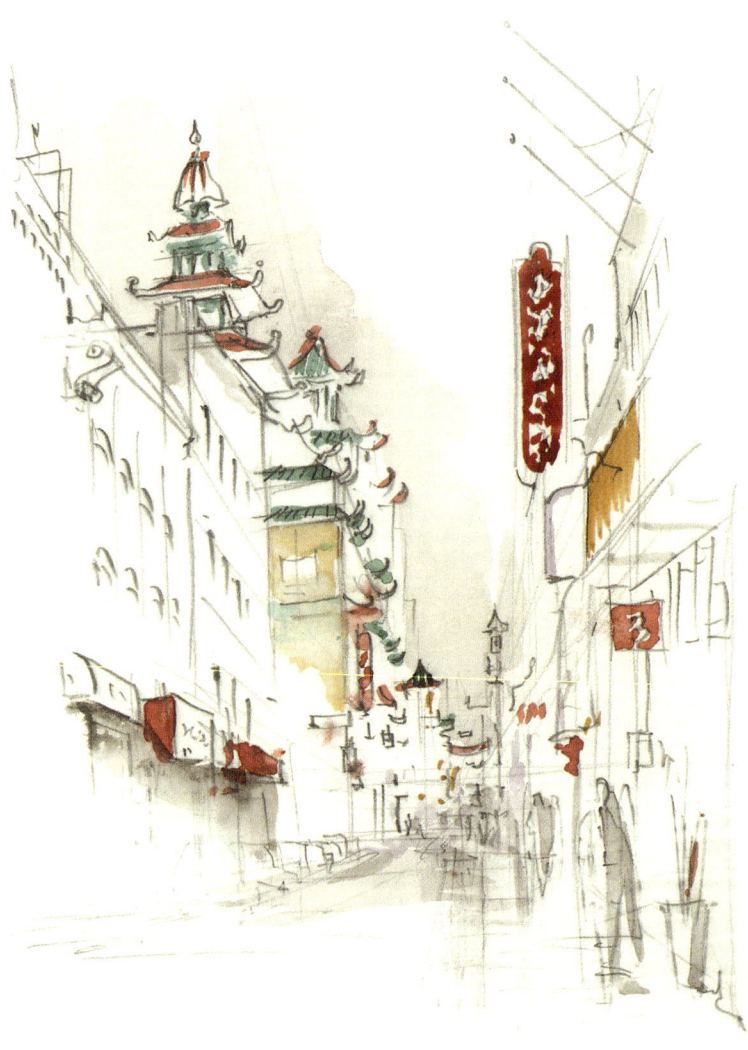

Chinatown is only a neighborhood, but it is one that, like Beijing's Forbidden City, delineates itself from the rest of the city by means of precise borders. It is not forbidden to go in, shop, look around, but no one who is not Chinese will understand what is being said, written, shouted, advised. The walls of Chinatown are not walls of stone, but walls of voices.

Recipe | Take one pyramid, Egyptian is fine. Grasp its top with your thumb and forefinger. Then pull up, stretching the point as if it were a piece of very elastic rubber. Pull higher, higher, and higher, until its height is at least ten times the width of one side of the base. Prick it with dozens of windows all alike. Then add two ears: the concrete elevator shafts. Lift everything up and place it on a small forest of intertwining pillars. Now take this building and drop it from above into the center of town right at the foot of Columbus Avenue. There you have it: you have made the Transamerica Pyramid, the most recognizable building in the city, a real icon, and not a bad one at that.

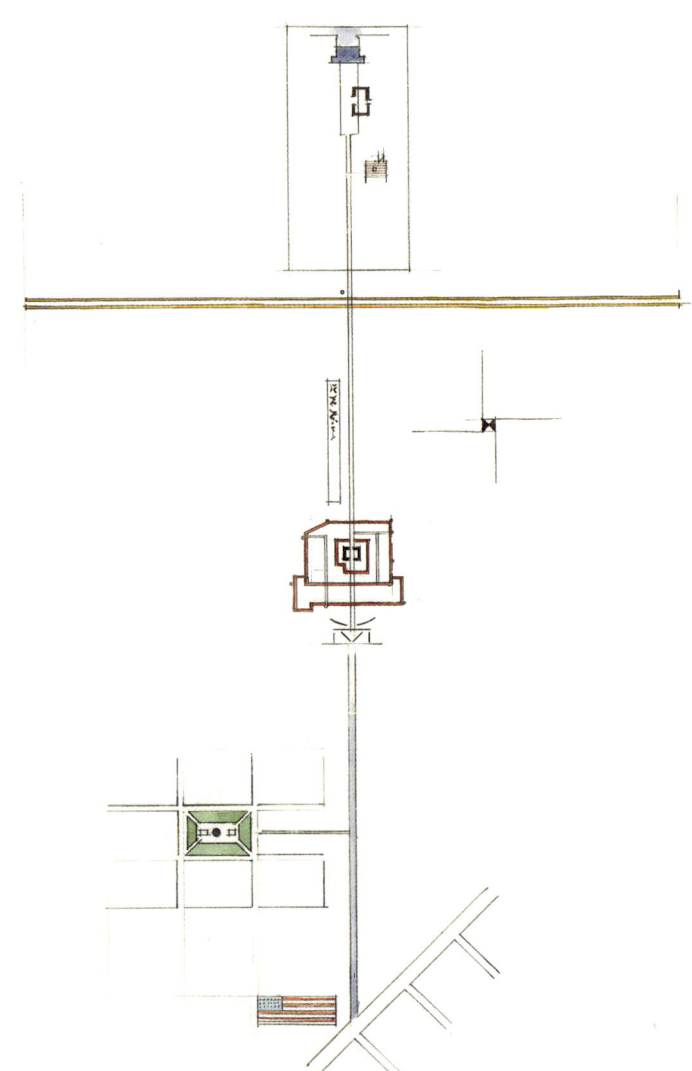

Columbus Tower (Sentinel Building) | Built
shortly after the 1906 earthquake on the corner of
Columbus and Kearny Street, in recent years it has
seen at least two of its records fall: that of being the
recognizable symbol of the area between North Beach
and Chinatown, a role taken over by the Transamerica
Pyramid; and, after the 2005 reconstruction of the
de Young Museum, that of being the only completely
copper-clad building in town.

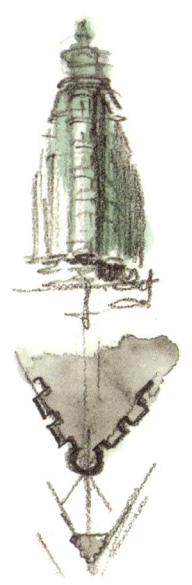

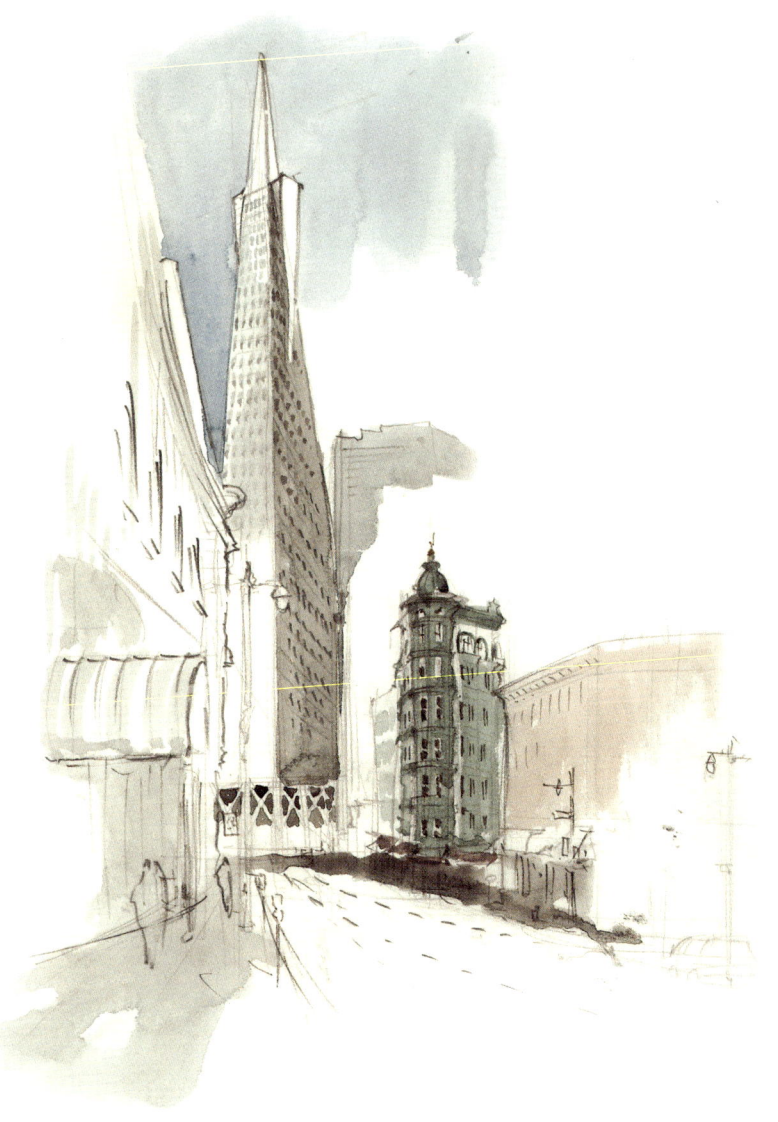

It is a Victorian flat iron, not exactly flat because its acute angle consists of a continuous cylindrical bow window six stories high, topped by a round turret. The copper sheathes it almost completely, conforming to the classical outlines of the architectural forms. Stamped with countless decorative motifs, the copper has turned a beautiful deep green made dense by an authentic patina that shows its history.

The Columbus Tower is an intimate urban building, a small high-rise built with grace and decorum. An architecture that, like its green copper sheathing, ages genteelly, increasing in elegance as time goes by.

Downtown 1 | Grant Avenue, first Italian, then Chinese, becomes purely American once past the pagoda-shaped gate that marks the boundary of Chinatown. Downtown begins.

The street is mainly commercial. Shops, showrooms, restaurants, lights, and signs.

First sign: "Avant cards." Greeting cards, apparently avant-garde.

Second sign: "Wine Bar." Gourmet Europe arrived here some years ago, but "wine bar," strangely, despite California wines, still recalls Rome or Paris more than here.

Third sign: "Banana Republic." Authentically American.

Fourth sign: "Wester Gallery." Picasso, Chagall, Dali, Matisse, and other names. Real art, but here interior decoration.

Fifth sign: "Public Parking." It would not be easy to get all the way here without these helpful buildings.

Sixth sign: "Prada." A little bit of Italy? By now not even that. A globalized street. A little piece of a world that is all alike.

Maiden Lane | The most intimate space, the kernel inside which, well-protected, is a seed from which the whole city seems to develop, is a little building, a gift shop turned art gallery. It is on Maiden Lane, an alley hidden in the heart of downtown. On its broad, spare brick façade, at lower left, on a red rectangle as in a Japanese print, is the architect's signature: Frank Lloyd Wright. Even the semicircular portal carved into the façade has an Oriental look, but also a classical, Roman one, with its bricks fanning out in a wide arch.

The entrance is deep like a tunnel to a secret cavern. At the end of the tunnel a small miracle appears: a long white ramp spirals upward, embracing the space with a gesture that is at once intimate and grand. This spiral would go on to become, on the opposite coast, in New York, the great conch shell of the Guggenheim Museum.

Once again, the beginning is in California. In the center of San Francisco, in a little brick cave, Frank Lloyd Wright found the stimulus to create an unprecedented vision, the opportunity for a new and courageous experience.

Towers | The highest, most massive and elegant tower downtown is the Bank of America building: a diamond-faceted prism, a redwood made of granite, whose bark consists of dug-out wedges that groove its exterior walls all the way up. The material is rich, solid, and dark (granite), its form an archetype (the monolith). The Bank of America Center is the male skyscraper, the king, the boss.

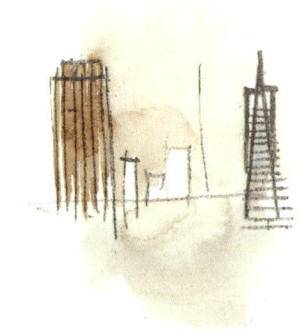

A short distance away rises its lady, the Transamerica Pyramid, slender and svelte. This building is more frivolous, light, genteel, but also daring and brave.

Despite the forest of high-rises that have been built all around them, they are still the king and queen reigning, unchallenged, over downtown.

Embarcadero Freeway | An architect friend of mine told me, in the long-ago 1980s, that speeding into downtown San Francisco on the Embarcadero Freeway was one of the most exciting experiences he had ever had. The Embarcadero exit was the last turnoff before the elevated freeway entered onto the Bay Bridge in the direction of East Bay. Drivers felt as if they were riding a hyperurban roller coaster, flying along for at least a mile in the midst of skyscrapers very close at hand until, after a broad curve, they glided into the heart of North Beach. Seen from the ground, the freeway had a completely different flavor: it was an incongruous, Brutalist wilderness of enormous concrete pilings, a barrier separating downtown from the front along the bay. The long piers and the beloved Ferry Building were cut off from the rest of the city, relegated to a narrow space, wedged in between the freeway and the sea.

The freeway ended at North Beach, but the idea of its original designers was to continue it all the way to the Golden Gate Bridge. This would have meant six miles of uninterrupted destruction of the most beautiful waterfront in America. The advantage was that it would save motorists the inconvenience of having to pass through the residential areas of North Beach, Russian Hill, and the Marina. A potential premeditated urban murder, this insane plan was luckily never carried out. Nonetheless, the local people have had to

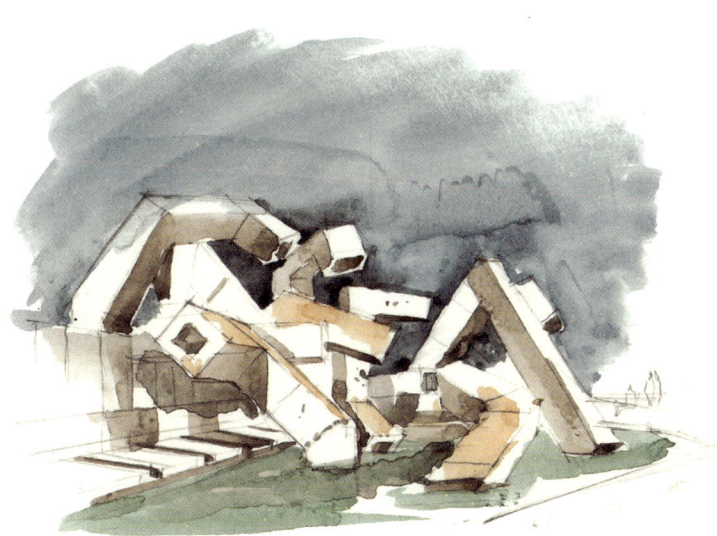

live for at least thirty years with this unfinished monument to ugliness. Finally, to Nature's great honor, the 1989 earthquake shook its foundations, cracked its massive concrete pilings, and made the freeway unusable. It could have been repaired and restored to its original function, but to no one's sorrow, the decision was made to tear it down completely. I was not in San Francisco at the time, but I would have enjoyed watching its demolition. Only now do I realize that the nearby fountain designed by Armand Vaillancourt, made up of a pile of broken pillars, foreshadowed, with visionary imagination, the ruins of the torn-down freeway.

Now it is finally possible to admire a civilized waterfront with palm trees and sidewalks, tram lines, streetlights, flower beds, and benches. It is an acceptable and well-built project, even if, in my opinion, it indulges in traditionalist prettiness. In any case, it is interesting to note that a removal, an absence, has re-created a place. Architecture and urban planning often involve acts of subtraction, not addition. It is an act of pure planning to choose what to subtract from the city, which buildings to tear down, what to eliminate, including trees, signals, billboards, and so on—maybe even putting the proposals up for a vote to verify the expectations and desires of the population. Residents know the city intimately by virtue of living there every day, and their evaluations of a project could bring this experience to bear. The risk is that superficial pragmatism could prevail, that fine buildings steeped in the history of the city could be torn down by popular demand. Power to the people or power to art? This is an old question that luckily, since everyone was in agreement, was not even posed in the case of the Embarcadero Freeway.

Downtown 2 | Looking up high. On the hundredth floor of the skyscrapers crowding in around me like a forest of silent prisms, many lights are still on. Mixed with the dark of the sky, these immense solids converge in perspective on a vanishing point at the zenith above me. One intuits that those millions of cubic meters of space are now empty. That all of the people who were there until a short while ago are now in the BART trains, lined up on the freeways, or drinking in the bars during happy hour.

Here below, the last headlights of the cars streak by. They, too, are thinning out. By 7:00 p.m., these streets that a few hours earlier were dense with noise, street vendors, beggars, and businessmen are deserted. Just

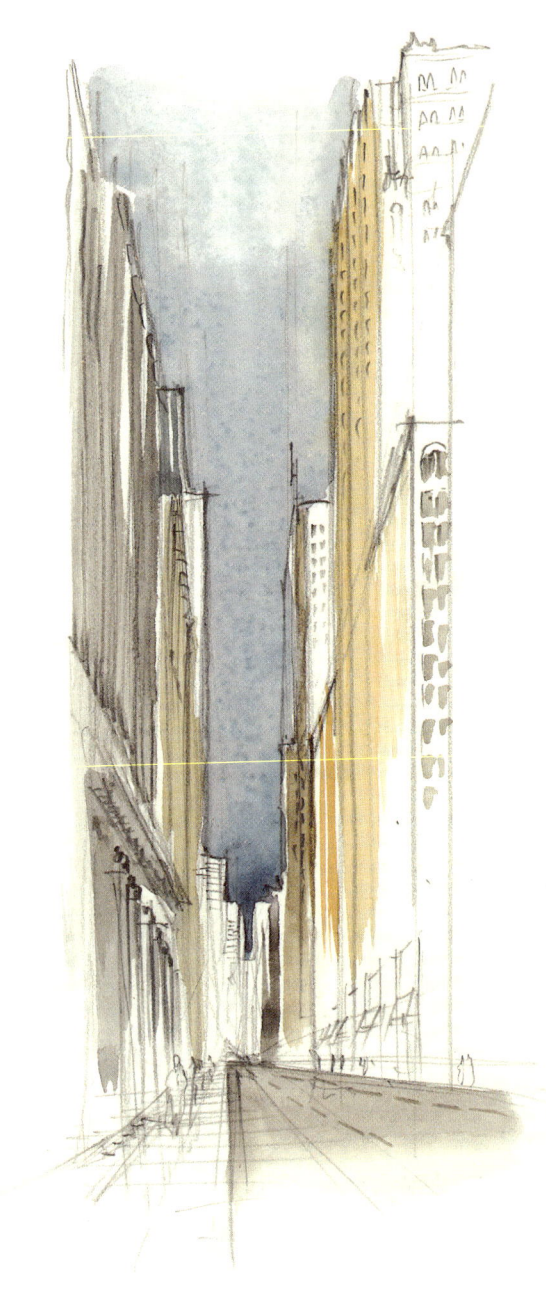

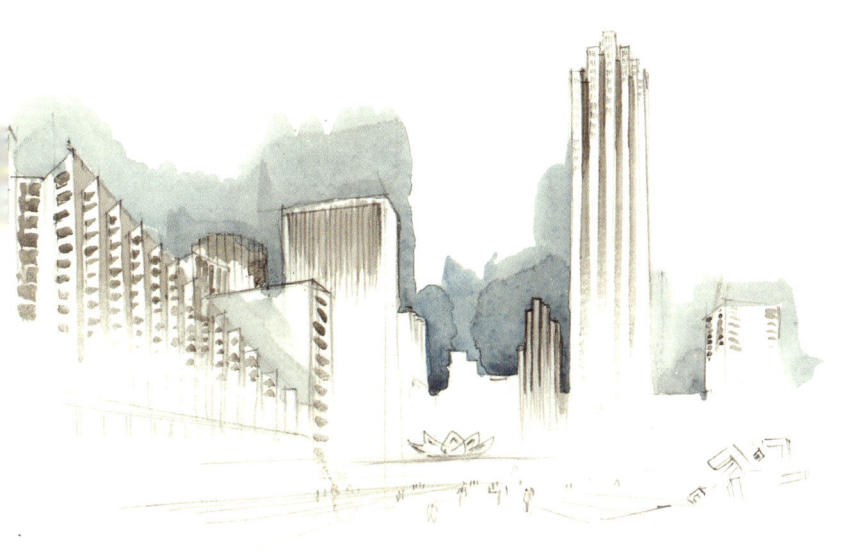

a few solitary passersby remain, or a homeless person heading for his cardboard pallet inside an entrance hallway. A streetcar passes, clacking on the rails; a horn blows in the distance. Only the traffic lights continue to play their part in an empty theater.

Half | Nestled on the end of a peninsula, San Francisco is divided into two parts: one open to the ocean and the other facing the bay. The boundary line is not sharply defined, but changes slightly according to the season, the direction of the wind, or the time of day. It is a purely meteorological division created by the presence or absence of fog. Many daily or permanent life decisions are dictated by this division: whether or not to put on a jacket before going out, where to go on a Sunday picnic, in what neighborhood to rent or buy a house.

Half the city lives in the ocean fog; half shines in the sunlight of the bay.

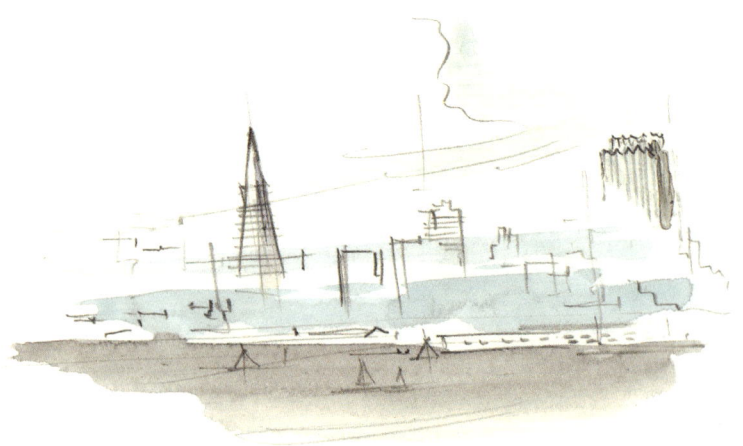

Half is gray and dark like the dark green of its trees; half is white with light, blue like the sea.

Half is damp, cold, silent; half is open, warm, full of light.

Half is the invisible, introverted, mysterious city; half is the visible city, wide open, serene.

On the Bay | The sea mixes with the clouds, the clouds become white islands, the islands green clouds, the land blue sky, the sea merges with the fog, and the sky turns into emerald-green water.

From Berkeley | Seen from Berkeley, the city is a barely perceptible profile of high-rises, a ziggurat emerging from the iron tangle of the Bay Bridge. Seen from here, San Francisco is a silhouette city, not white and luminous as it appears from Sausalito or Tiburon, but gray and metallic like the bridge and freeways that lead to it. From here, the Marin Hills are far away, and even farther still and invisible is the ocean, with its cold breezes and its fog.

Sausalito | I have stopped by the side of the road that runs along the bay just outside of Tiburon before getting onto the freeway for San Francisco. It is early in the morning. There is fog, not the thick fog that doesn't let you see three feet in front of you, but the fog that hides the horizon.

There is a little meadow in front of me, then the gray tremble of water that turns into sky without a boundary line. Beyond the water, I know, are Sausalito and the hills. Now there is only the dense, damp gray that hides everything.

What is inside the fog? The fog is like our future. What will follow the present? Maybe the same things that we know, just barely different. Time will go by, and the sun will little by little burn away the fog, and the coast here before me will reappear. For now, though, reality is a gray cloak. Only the houses and meadow nearby and my present are real and visible, only the birds hopping on the hedge in front of me, only this hand that is writing. I don't know if, when the fog goes away, Sausalito, the trees, and the boats will be real and visible, if I will still be here watching the hills appear beyond the bay. Perhaps I will already be gone, off to other places.

65 Miles per Hour | Gliding along at 65 miles per hour toward San Francisco, with the roar of the engine in the background, on the freeway that runs along above Sausalito: a wide curve with the other cars, companions on the descent toward the tunnel. A mile

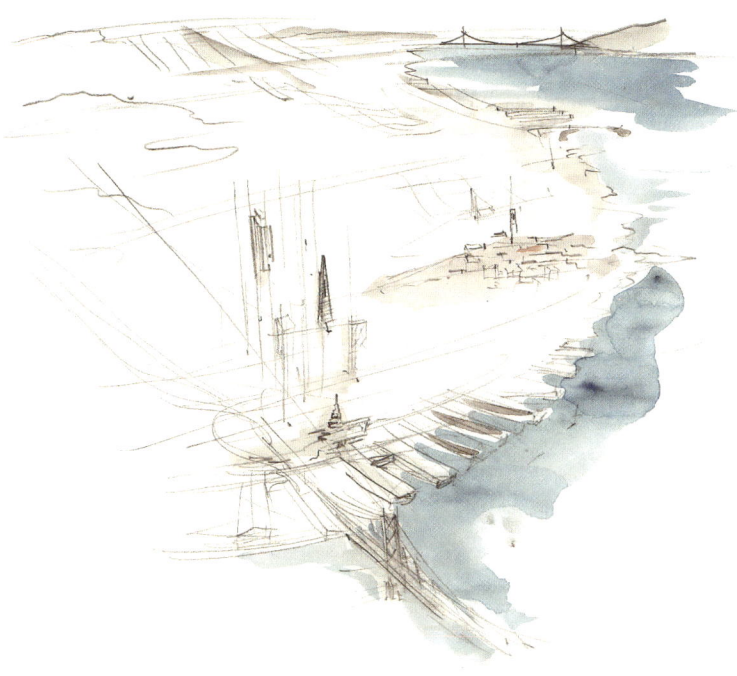

dug out of the rock, then light and the big bridge. The
noise grows denser, to the beat of the short, abrupt
bumps of the expansion joints in the paving. At the
edges of the road, the vertical cables of the bridge hang
down like the strings of a giant harp, and the ocean
flows past the rails of the red parapet like the frames
of an old silent movie.

I have to slow down—"pay toll"—30 mph, then 20, 10—"six dollars"—"thank you"—"you're welcome"— "toll paid"—go—30, 50, 60 miles per hour, I pick up speed coming onto Lombard Street, a wide, urban, six-lane boulevard. I hope to catch all the green lights, all twenty of them, stretching into the distance. I pass at least five or six lights without having to stop; then click, one turns a predictable red. Speed: 0 mph. I start up again and get to an intersection. Stop. The cars pass one at a time, according to the order of their arrival.

The street narrows. It starts uphill again on Russian Hill, grows steeper. The engine automatically shifts gears, roars, pushes, pulls. At the first intersection the street flattens again for a few meters, then starts to climb. One could start to feel dizzy and afraid that the car might stop and slide back down the hill. One more gasp and we reach the top. It is the climax of a motoring orgasm, finally at the summit. From here one has a view of the bay and downtown. The tops of the highrises are as high as my car and I, here on the hill.

The flat area doesn't last long, and the road starts downhill in a descent so steep it seems vertical. One has to believe: in the car engine, the brakes, the automatic transmission. Have no fear. Come down slowly, keep the car in low gear, hold back on the reins like you're guiding a mule down a steep mountain path. A few more meters and the vertigo is over: finally a crosswalk as the street relaxes into a gentle slope. I draw a breath, silently thanking the car, engine, transmission, emergency brake for performing well on this high-altitude trek.

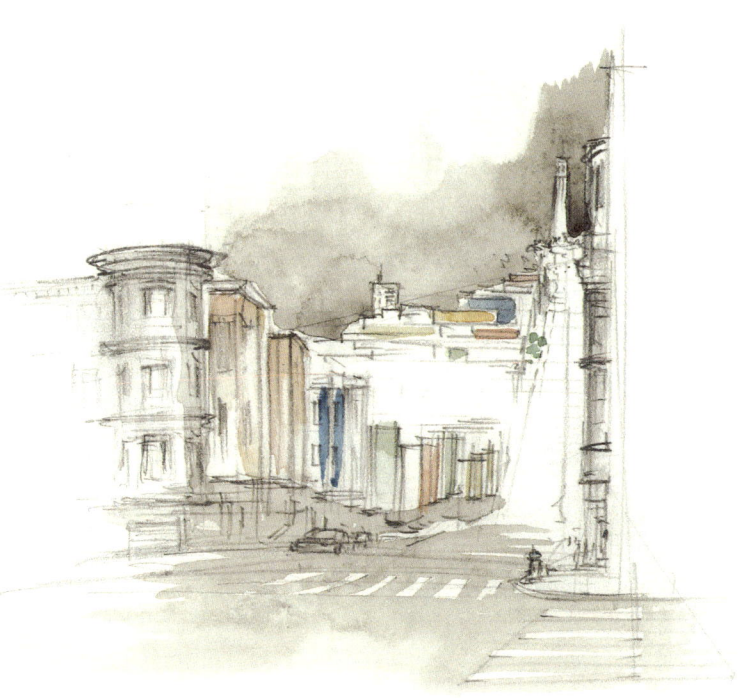

Tide | The water in the bay withdraws, leaving visible a slimy beach two or three times bigger than the real beach. This is the 9:00 a.m. low tide. The same effect will appear with the low tide at 6:00 p.m. Every day the bay demonstrates, to anyone who pays even a little attention, that the earth is living and breathing, that just as Leonardo da Vinci said, it is a vital body, with its own autonomous rhythms, its lungs, heart, blood, bones, and skin.

Alcatraz | Alcatraz is an abandoned ship, a Flying Dutchman set adrift that bears the signs of a life of torment.

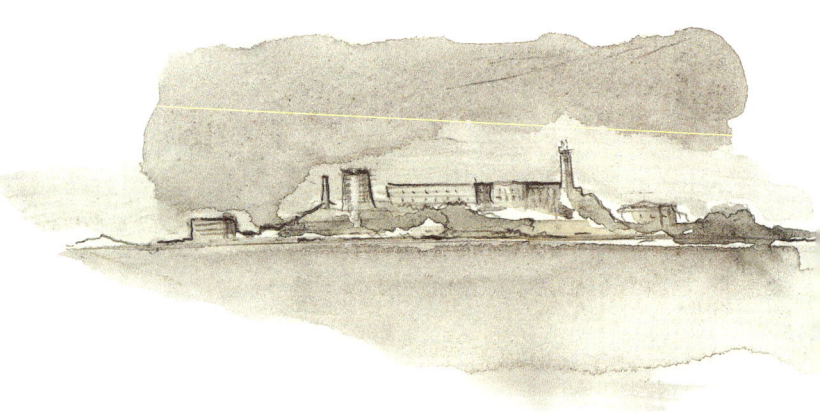

When it was inhabited by the living, it was the island of Death Row. Even before that, it was a bare island, a free-standing rock at the mercy of the wind and the waves, a refuge for seagulls, maybe for pelicans. Alcatraz = pelican: a toponymic irony, the name of a free seabird given to an island of prisoners.

Once the prison was closed, the question was: what to do with Alcatraz? A museum, a sanctuary for birds and seals, even a gambling casino; or leave it as it is, with its austere prison buildings? This last option won out. After all, Alcatraz is the San Francisco monument most visited by tourists. Why pass up the income to be earned from those who flock there to shudder, safely, at sensational stories of crime?

Colors | San Francisco is white, green, and gray.

White like the houses glittering in the sun when you look at the city from Sausalito or Mount Tamalpais.

Green like the Presidio woods damp with fog, the sunny field of Dolores Park, the frothy waters of the bay in a stiff wind.

Gray like the fog that wraps around it, cools it, hides it.

Wires | They look like the threads of a spider web, left hanging here since the pioneers' time. Couldn't a vulture perch on these T-shaped wooden light poles running along at least half of the streets in San Francisco? Aren't these the same poles that, lining the dirt roads across the western prairies, have come all the way here? Now the poles are corroded by the salt air, bleached by the rain, punctured by the staples that have held thousands of flyers, layer after layer, palimpsests of events: rooms for rent, movies, massages, yoga lessons.

Skeins of wires run from one pole to another, dipping slightly in the middle of the road. They twist around ceramic insulation spools or metal pins sticking out from the fronts of the houses. Along those wires runs the energy that powers the vacuum cleaner, the hair dryer, the electric clock. Along those wires hanging over the streets runs the hidden life of the houses: the lighted screens, the lamps, the electric blankets, the coffeemaker every morning.

Pacific Heights | Pacific Heights, high on the Pacific, with the streets going down toward the water of the bay like the marks of a comb that has caressed the hillside or the furrows of a tractor in a plowed field.

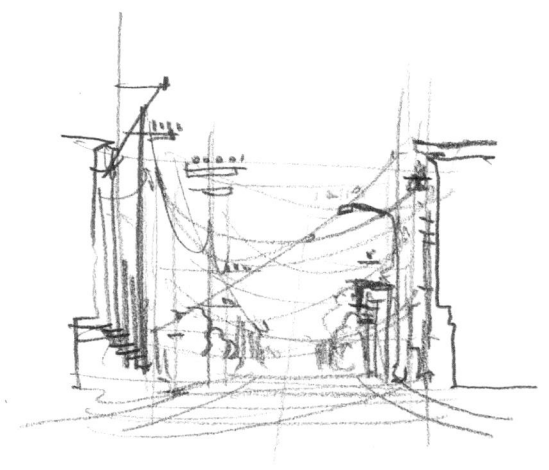

Pacific Heights is a plateau from which one can watch the shipping traffic. The ships pass slowly, islands in motion, next to Alcatraz, a real island that looks like a ship with its portholes and smokestacks.

Along the streets are mansions in various styles: Tudor, Georgian, French Hotel, Palladian, Colonial. The sunsets are beautiful beyond the windows of the beautiful houses; the fireplaces are burning in the well-appointed living rooms. Well-tended are the flowers in the yards, polished the Jaguars and BMWs in the garages.

71

Finis Terrae | There is an old windmill looking onto Ocean Beach, right at the edge of the Golden Gate Park. It was built to pump freshwater to the trees in the park. The windmill faces west, the open sea, ready to defy the wind and salt air, to accumulate the energy that comes from the Pacific. The windmill breathes energy to fuel its sails. It seems to stand there to tell us what to do: to set our eyes on a cleaner nature, to look into the distance, to breathe the sea.

Ocean Beach | Today, at Ocean Beach, is a great day for surfing. It's early, but a bright sun already is lighting up the beach. It is a wonderful Sunday morning for those black-suited bodies that float far from shore in the middle of the sea. Long waves, high walls of water that swell up to break on themselves. Little dark-colored bodies, human amphibians lying on their boards, wait floating beyond the breakers where the water is still calm. They are waiting for the big wave, the one that will become high, strong, powerful. Here it comes. Hands paddle the water, the board picks up speed, the surfer stands up seeking his balance. His body bends, the board cuts diagonally through the water, fleeing the foam chasing it, glides along until the wave loses strength and the body crumples into the water.

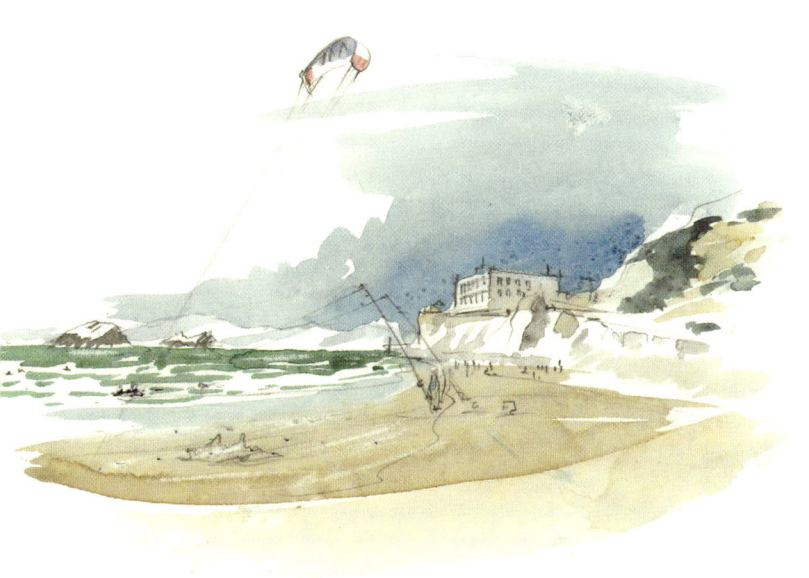

The waves continue to form, swell, break, one after the other against Ocean Beach, against the coast. From a distance, from the beach, comes a drumbeat. The rhythm of the wave, of sound, of life, the rhythm of time.

People Have Drowned Here | *People swimming and wading have drowned here.* Then, underneath: *Corrente peligrosas. Emergency 911. Danger: rip currents,* warns the sign on the sidewalk along Ocean Beach.

You can die swimming in the water, while you are living the intensity of emotions. Riding a wave is a rodeo with nature. You can die from inexperience, or a physical problem, or countless other causes. You have to know this. You are alive and want to go swimming, but remember that death is always there, it has the body of the sea, the embrace of a wave; it is there, next to you, sensual and enveloping.

Finis Terrae 2 | Here ends San Francisco, here terminates America. Here ends Kerouac's journey, the journey of the old hippies, of the pioneers of long ago. Here ended some of the best minds of the generation of Allen Ginsberg and his friends: dead in the mud, cut down by drugs, worn out by AIDS. But here, too, ended up those who took off their chains and took them off others, who embraced each other and saw dharma. Here the "best minds" ended up, to produce ideas, poetry, utopias, images, films, computers. Here ends the West. Beyond the rotundity of the ocean is the East. But do we still breathe the air coming from over there? Do we still breathe the creative doubt, the search without creeds, the Tao and Zen, Bashō's poems, the words of Chuang Tzu, Confucius, Lao Tzu?

Golden Gate Park | The eucalyptus tree twists around itself. It is a restless old man with jagged skin. His bark is a thin sheet, white, gray, and beige, a sheet shredded in the storms. He constantly sheds his skin, which piles up at his feet, entangling with the leaves scattered on the ground. Many disparage the eucalyptus as a weed (maybe the same people who call pigeons "flying rats"). For me, it is a sensitive and restless tree, a delicate friend.

Right next to it rises a pine tree, an autochthonous tree that is native here. With the eucalyptus and the redwood, it is a tree that symbolizes California. Evergreen, it has a powerful, contorted trunk that splits into many sharp-pointed and somewhat disorderly branches. The branches sustain tufts of green needles that hang, like Oriental trees, suspended in the air like a pagoda. Growing along the coast, it has messy hair, the branches often dead or broken off.

I do not see one, but somewhere around here there is surely a redwood. The redwood is the tree most emblematic of this part of America: a mysterious, primitive being, come down from the mountains to reach all the way to the sea. There is a dense, dark forest enclosed in a damp valley, just a few miles beyond the Golden Gate: Muir Woods. It is a fairy-tale forest, a green temple with tall, tall columns, fluted by time and by the fog that is practically perennial there. The redwood is a fir tree, and the tallest tree in the world. The redwood forests provided the wood to build the houses of California. Now it is a protected tree, its wood expensive and highly prized. Hugging a redwood was an act of love in the 1960s and 1970s, when the hippies found their perfect humus in the redwood forests of Marin County and Big Sur.

The Academy of Sciences and the de Young | The de Young Museum and the Academy of Sciences face each other. Their long walls delimit the space of the park-plaza that was already there, a sort of San Francisco Tuleries inside Golden Gate Park.

The de Young is a solid mass, a rough but elegant body, faceted but compact. The Academy of Sciences is an ethereal, transparent building, lace made of glass and slender columns.

The de Young is a geological block, a biological body, a metal animal. The Academy is a technological, Cartesian machine, a perfect parallelepiped.

The de Young has a single organic skin, a layer of perforated copper, iridescent, changeable with the weather. The Academy has a skin made of layers: concrete, glass, and painted iron. Always the same.

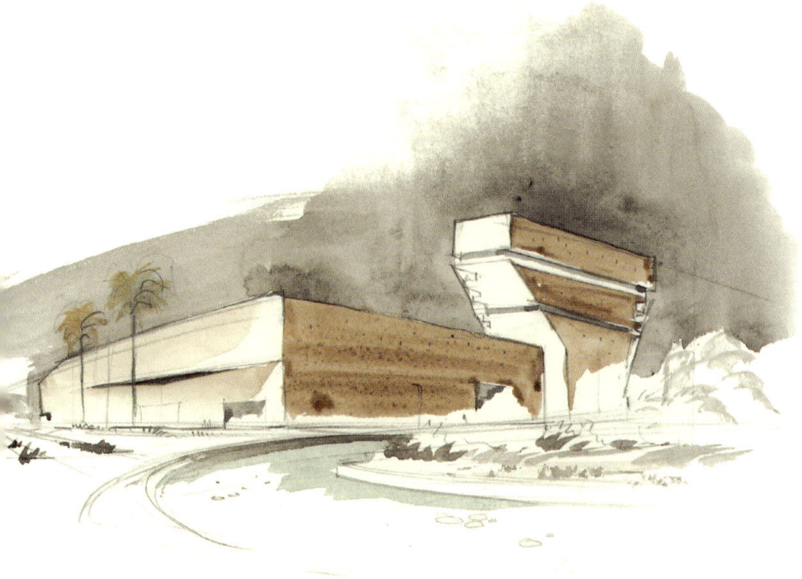

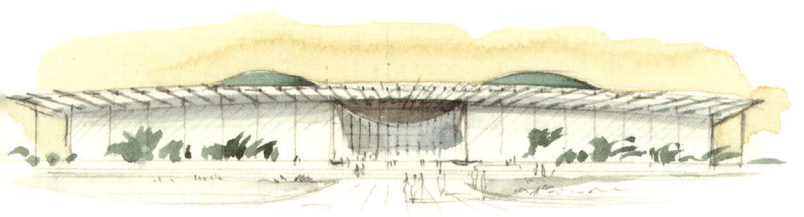

The de Young is sculptural with its tower and the great protrusion of the roof jutting toward the park. Its geometry plays on the contrast between straight and slanted lines. The Academy is symmetrical, light, and evanescent, an orthogonal space interrupted only by the rotund artificial organic roof. Its geometry plays completely on the contrast between straight line and curve.

At the de Young, the entrance is low, horizontal, a hole in the façade that leads into a spare, simple, semi-enclosed courtyard. At the Academy, the entrance is the principal element, its heart, the center, tall, transparent, and luminous, of the complex.

The de Young exudes a sense of suprahuman grandeur, of a silent, austere space. The Academy is a fair of sounds, light effects, bodies in motion, a festival of life and color.

And yet, perhaps precisely because of these differences, the two buildings integrate well with each other and their overall context. If anything, it is the plaza in front of them that lacks their strength. Its nineteenth-century look relates only to the great exedra that bounds it on the west. As to the rest, with its little avenues, fountains, and circles of trees, it hinders rather than helps the dialogue between the two protagonists.

Buffaloes | In the park, there is a large fenced pasture in which buffaloes graze. They look like bulls, but more hunchbacked, hairier, like bulls wearing fur. This was the land of Indians and buffaloes. Now only a few remain: most have been wiped out, the Native Americans as well as the buffaloes. The animals graze in their fenced pasture, no longer even desiring to escape.

Copper | The copper skin of the de Young Museum adapts perfectly to the context of the park. The museum is an animal that camouflages itself in the green of the trees, in the broken roots, the bark of the tree trunks scattered on the damp ground. It is a whale come out of the sea, an animal left lying on the ground when the waters of a flood recede. A monster whose mouth is still breathing the oxygen of the nearby woods. The bodies sitting under the roof-palate at the open-air cafeteria look like lots of little Jonahs. Like Moby Dick, different from any other sea monster because of its color, the de Young, a portentous animal, has a skin different from any other: pocked and for this reason more resistant; perforated and because of this more varied and variable; a skin that changes color, that is alive, that responds, like the bark of the trees, to the constant changes in the light, the air, the weather.

79

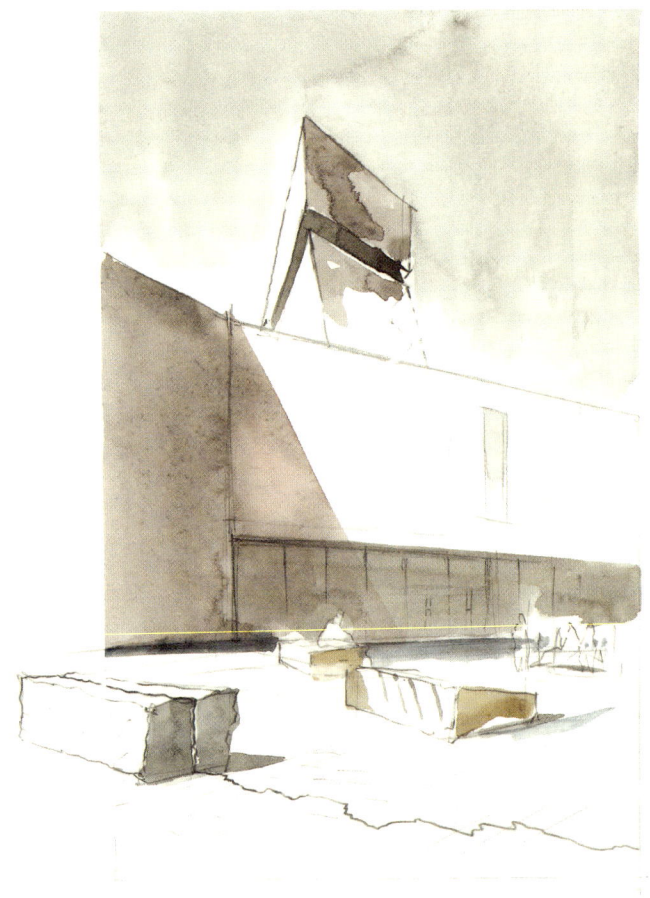

The Crack | The thin crack that accompanies anyone from the moment they enter the plaza of the de Young Museum is a metaphor. Among the many possible interpretations of this environmental sculpture, one prevails: this is the fissure on which the entire place is sitting, the subtle disconnect that pervades the city, its surroundings, the fault that threatens the entire state of California, that rises from the entrails of the earth to emerge silent, pervasive, ineluctable on the surface. The crack moves from the earth to our bodies, enters our soul; it can upset us suddenly, just as, suddenly, the force that lies waiting only for the moment to strike can shake itself up from the depths.

Classicism-Modernism | In the apron in front of the California Palace of the Legion of Honor, there is a large sculpture made of iron girders painted red and welded together to form a sort of big letter *K*: an abstract sculpture. In the background, the perfectly symmetrical palace, a sort of Greek agora surrounded by classical columns, with a great triumphal arch in the center decorated by marble bas-reliefs depicting the Muses. The positioning of the abstract sculpture in front of the Classical building creates an undeniable and certainly deliberate contrast: they have nothing in common, not their period, their style, color, material, geometry, spirit, or any symbolic relationship. These spatial-artistic oxymorons are frequent in San Francisco and, to a certain extent, all over America. Maybe even more frequent than in Europe.

Not far from here is the Palace of Fine Arts: a sort of Pantheon surrounded by an enormous exedra of Corinthian columns. The complex looks like a mastodonic urban ruin of an ancient villa or Classical temple. The composition is in reality the façade of a humble, albeit also grand, space behind it, made of iron beams and a tin roof: a "decorated shed" which until 2013 housed the Exploratorium, an interactive physics museum, the complete opposite of the Palace of Fine Arts also in terms of function.

There are other cases of similar architectural contrasts: Grace Cathedral, for example, the Neo-Gothic cathedral of San Francisco, is a Californian Notre Dame sunk into a square surrounded by Rationalist high-rises. Or the Beaux-Arts composition of the Civic Center flanked by the contemporary Modernist semi-arches of the Opera House and the Federal Building.

Here, too, as elsewhere, Classicism and Modernism stand next to each other in a symbiosis that, to me, never seems perfectly resolved. One senses a certain mutual incomprehension, perhaps indifference, in their uneasy coexistence.

Hills | Nob, Russian, Telegraph, Portrero are Hills. Pacific is an aristocratic Height. Of the more or less forty-three high or low hills that are said to make up the city of San Francisco, one surpasses all the others in height. Neither a Hill nor a Height, it is something more: a Peak, or rather much more: Twin Peaks.

Coastlines | Do this little exercise: look at a map of San Francisco and describe the shape of the boundary line between the city and the water.

Start from the docks by Bay Bridge: Don't all those piers that jut into the sea one after the other like the spread fingers of a hand look like the horizontal projections of all the skyscrapers nearby? It is as though the skyline of downtown San Francisco had flipped over 90 degrees onto the water of the bay. "Skyline" of the tall high-rises, "sealine" of the long piers.

The perpendicular profiles of the coastline of the piers tilt more and more the closer one gets to Fisherman's Wharf. On the map, they create a sort of architectonic fan. To be sure, the change in direction is due to the need to position them optimally with respect to the movement of the waves in the bay, following the curve of the peninsula at that point to keep the waves from hitting the boats broadside that are tied up there. After the Fisherman's Wharf marina, the piers disappear, making way for a real port with a pier extending in a semicircle into the bay.

Continuing on our way, after a brief promontory, three new piers stretch out once again in an orderly fashion into the bay: this is the Fort Mason complex. Then the coast assumes the aspect of a straight line along the grassy fields of the Marina. Another harbor for yachts, and finally a long, straight beach that was once the site of the Crissy Field military base and is now open to the public. The beach narrows and vanishes shortly before encountering the pylons of the Golden Gate Bridge.

From here on, the coast changes aspect and direction. The bay turns into ocean, and the line that up to now was man-made turns into a rocky cliff turning sharply to the south. Another beach, and then, in a zigzag of inlets and promontories, we come to Point Lobos, the westernmost point of the entire territory. Here the little islands of Seal Rocks break off from the mainland.

As though wanting to rest after all this zigzagging, the coastline grows flat again and stretches out at Ocean Beach. A long, wide beach that goes on for

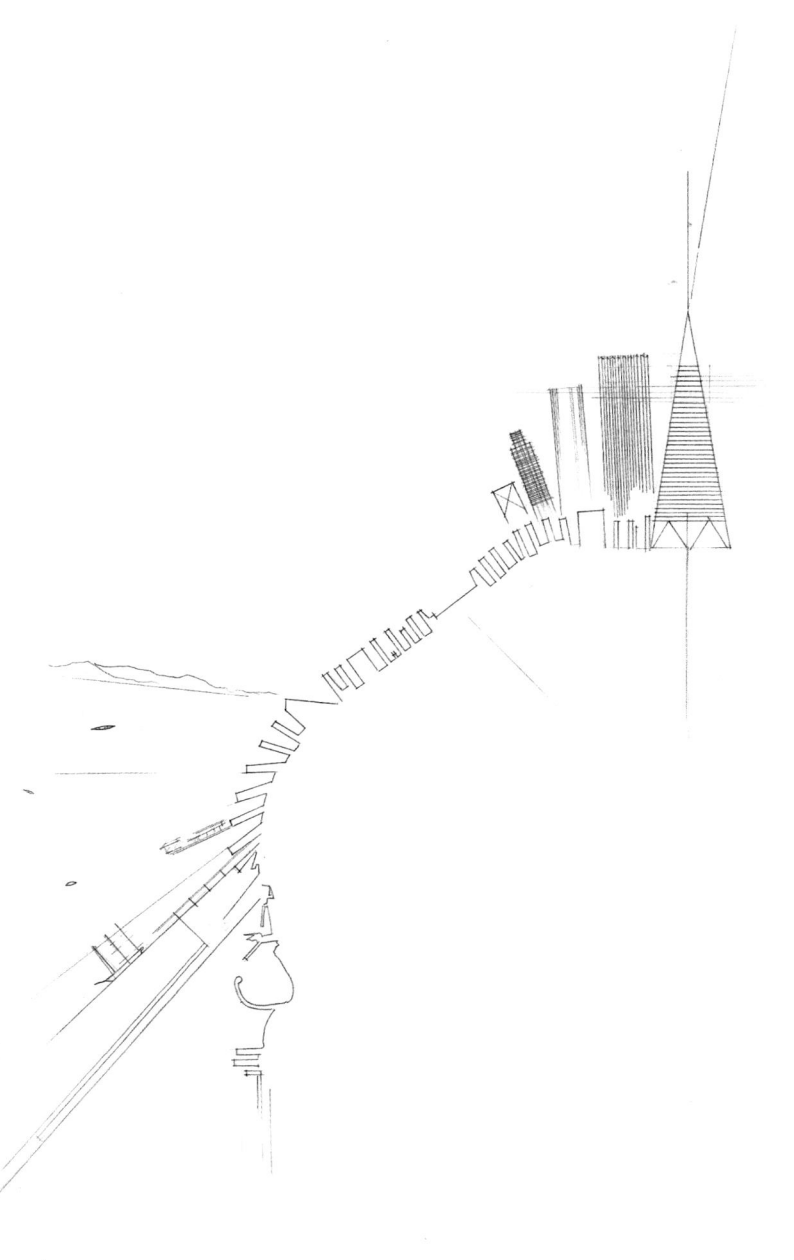

miles before turning into wild dunes. This is the end
of San Francisco. Off the map, the coastline continues
its course southward, designing the profile of the entire
state of California.

Downey Street | A short little street in the Haight-
Ashbury area, Downey Street climbs up a hill as though
looking for a point from which to embrace the pan-
orama of the whole city, from the ocean to North Beach.

Downey Street is tree-lined, and every tree is different. So, too, is every house, but all of them are at the
most three stories tall. Some have a flat roof, others
a pointed roof, designed like a little temple. In the
triangular tympanum, behind a little window, is the
attic, the highest room in the house, the most intimate,
the one that in earlier times served as storage space,
but often now has been transformed into a cozy little
bedroom where one can barely stand up, and only in
the middle of the room.

The façades of the houses are a carnival of colors,
a wooden fantasy of bow windows, dormer windows,
terraces, front porches, columns, carved wood, railings. Sometimes the fronts are covered with square or
rounded wooden shingles, other times by narrow horizontal boards or panels framed like an old-fashioned
wardrobe.

A tiny fissure separates each house from the one next door. It is a sharp division, as high and deep as the entire building. There are no party walls. I suppose that this separation is intended to protect against earthquake damage, but perhaps it is meant to showcase the individual style of each house. Does anything ever fall into that narrow one- or two-inch space? Does a cat ever get stuck as it tries to capture some animal? Who cleans this space? Who tends it?

Gated Communities | Along the winding roads of the Presidio, one often encounters big portals that indicate the presence of exclusive "gated communities," a term that does not make clear whether the bar across the road is meant to keep outsiders from coming in or to keep those inside from going out. Gated communities are one of the extreme forms of urban "defensible space." They are the sign of our desire to draw boundary lines, of our wish to live with those who are most like us, of the insecurity transmitted by the city. The consequence of their proliferation is the progressive erosion of public space in favor of private. One could say that gated communities tap a primeval need—don't all doors, gates, drawbridges have the same function? Don't they serve to protect from danger, to discourage intruders, to unite the besieged?

Garage Sale | The most inviolable part of the street is where the curb thins out and flattens to make it clear that you cannot park there: there is a garage here! "Tow away, day and night" is frequently posted on a sign. The garage is sacred space, even more than the front door. These edifices, even if they seem to date to a preindustrial time, were not built until car ownership had become widespread.

On the less commercial streets, every house has its own garage. For the owner, this is a great asset, because this means there are at least two parking places: one inside the garage and one in front of it. The garage also serves as a storage room, a sort of basement, and sometimes as a store on Saturday or Sunday morning when odds and ends are piled up for a garage sale. For one day this space, usually so tenaciously guarded, closed, and inaccessible, becomes a public space, an extension of the open street, available to everyone: passersby, browsers, and buyers.

Lower Haight | On every lamppost along the street someone has hung large printed banners informing us that we are on "Lower Haight," that is, the lower part of Haight Street. The banners announce that here we'll find life, fashion, commercial establishments, restaurants. Upper Haight, too, played its part in times gone by. Then it slowly petered out, first with the end of the Flower Power era, then with the AIDS epidemic in the 1980s. Could Lower Haight be the heir of the old, happy Haight Street? For now, it seems to me just a street like so many others around it: a few cafés, a couple of tattoo parlors, shops selling herbal remedies and organic foods. It should be said, however, that Haight Street, Noe Valley, Mission are still the areas where young people, kids, come to live; this is the San Francisco still fired by vision. To be sure, the crazy, transgressive exuberance that ran in the streets of that era is gone now, but at least San Francisco is still known as the city of fresh minds, the place that best represents the California spirit. Don't people say that the East Coast is the land of cynics, the Midwest of believers, and the West Coast is the land of seekers?

Dolores Park | If San Francisco had squares or plazas like European or Latin American cities, then the plaza that best reflects its identity would be Dolores Park. As its name indicates, it is a park, not a square. But not a park in the sense of a grassy field, sports facilities, and so on; it is a plaza-park because here one feels that there is still something of the *zócalo* and something of Europe.

The areas of the park are identifiable by their use

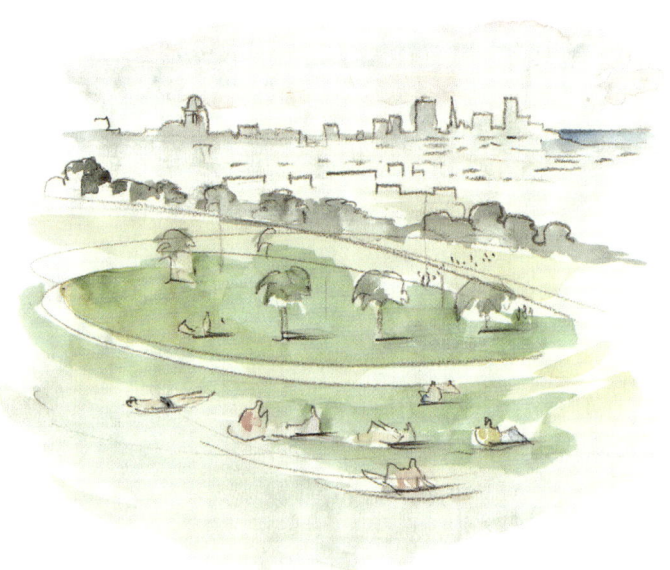

or by the ethnic groups that use them. It is Sunday morning. Up high is the lawn chosen by the gays; they sunbathe in swimsuits, even in the winter. Halfway up the hill, Hispanics are the majority; then there are groups of people squatting or sitting on the grass playing instruments, chatting, or exchanging some ethereal substance. Then there are the apprentice jugglers (with balls, sticks, or other paraphernalia). And families with children around a barbecue grill. There are people sleeping on the slope, throwing Frisbees to their dogs, climbing trees, stretching in the sun.

From here, the view takes in the whole city; the skyscrapers downtown, the Mexican bell towers, the Masonic domes, the palm trees of Los Angeles, the Victorian bow windows, and the East Bay Hills. The plaza-park runs downhill: a big grassy field that adapts to the hillside. It is square, and it is precisely this geometric shape that makes it a true "topographic square," analogous to the whole city of San Francisco, the topographic city par excellence, which, like a quilt of squares all the same size and shape, conforms to its up-and-down bed.

Market Street | If San Francisco were a valley, not a city, Market Street would be the main river into which its principal tributaries flowed. The ones on the right: all the streets from First to Seventeenth, as well as Guerrero, Dolores, Castro, etc. The ones on the left: Divisadero, Fillmore, and a hundred other streets including California Street. If Market Street is the Mississippi, California Street is its Missouri, a river that flows down to the valley marked by the wakes of the cable car rails.

Market Street is a wide, capacious river that cuts the city diagonally. Its source is on the heights of Twin

Peaks, and its course is studded with stores, houses, offices, palmettos, and period lampposts. Toward the estuary it becomes a gorge sunk in a canyon of skyscrapers. There it gathers gold and mud, businessmen and tramps with their shopping carts. There the Powell Street cable car finishes its run, while underground runs the karst river of the Bay Area Rapid Transit.

At the end of its course, however, Market Street is unable to flow into the waters of the bay. There is a dam: the Ferry Building. Its clock tower, ever since the 1989 earthquake eliminated the freeway that covered it up, once again functions as the visual focal point of the great diagonal street.

The Mint | I now realize where Walt Disney found his inspiration for Uncle Scrooge's castle-coffer. Right on the intersection of Market and Dolores stands the impregnable mass of the United States Mint. Its architecture is mighty and austere, with slanted walls three feet thick that rise up, like a medieval fortress, from a platform of rock deliberately left rough and stony. Here the treasury of America is minted. However, only the name "Mint" and an American flag waving from a mast indicate its owner and contents. There is no big dollar sign on the façade as on Uncle Scrooge's treasure chest.

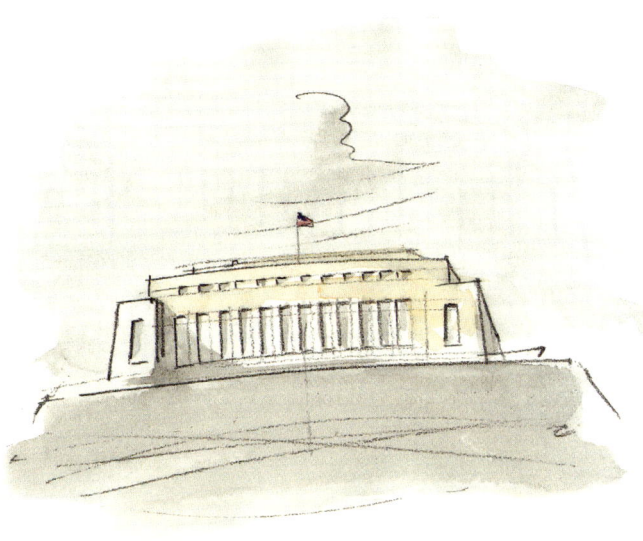

Homeless | An old man squatting by the side
of Market Street holds a piece of cardboard with
the hand-lettered sign: "Homeless—help." He leans
against a fence, behind which is a huge hole dug out of
the ground.

"Smith General Contractors" says the big sign, in
nicely printed lettering. Here will be built towers at
least thirty stories high: "360° views," "luxury pent-
houses," "fitness center," and other amenities. Maybe

the old man squatting there will go somewhere else tomorrow, when the bulldozer and steam shovels resume their work.

Tenderloin | The sin district: homeless wanderers, cheap hotels, strange bars, dusty neon signs. Tenderloin is a vital muscle, right in the center of town, a stone's throw from downtown and Pacific Heights. Tenderloin is a choice cut, but here it is soft, flaccid, maybe even gone a bit off. Precisely because of its derelict nature, it can call forth repugnance, pity, or an urge for social justice.

South of Market | South of Market. SoMa, as it is often called, could be a generic neighborhood in any American city: freeways crossing it elevated on massive pylons, under which square warehouse buildings are lined up; old brick buildings with hand-painted signs faded by time; the imprints of old cable car tracks swallowed up by new blacktopping; rolling shutters, big painted iron windows, wooden poles with bunches of electric wires attached to them, carts parked on the ramps going up to the lofts. But South of Market, like every urban industrial area in America, is changing, has already changed. First artists' studios, then home furnishings showrooms and new residential lofts

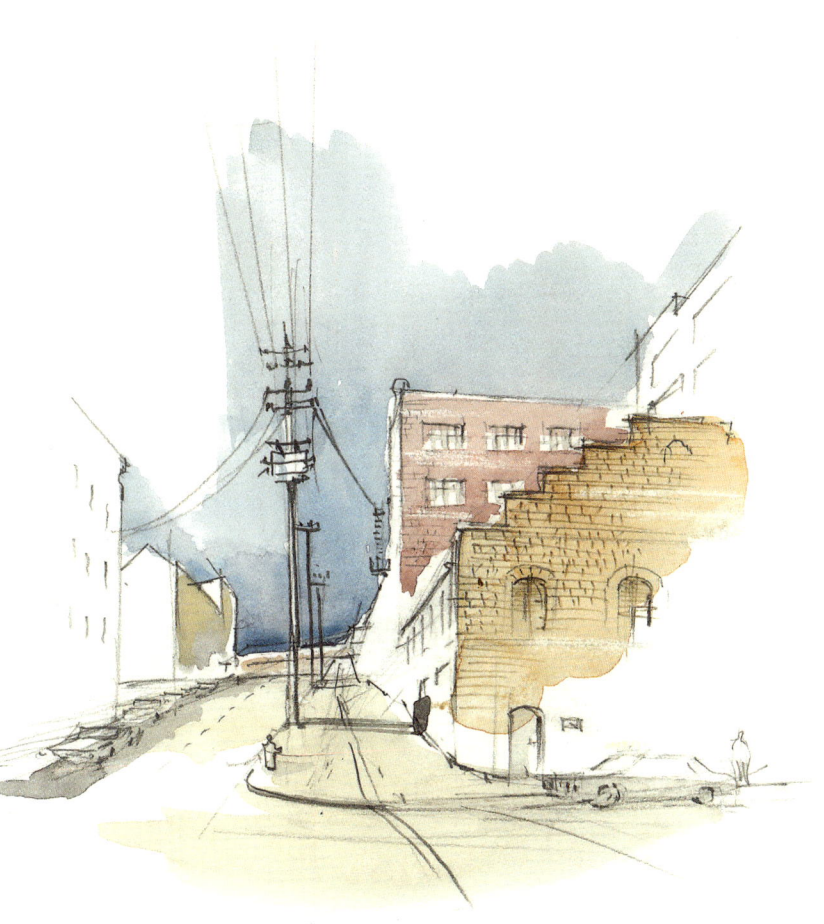

decorated with designer kitchens and fireplaces. The bulldozers have done their job. Many buildings have been torn down. Wonderful opportunities for young architects to experiment with new bow windows in glass, aluminum screens, Cor-ten steel railings. Thus new two- and three-story buildings have sprung up, often stylistically reminiscent of the old industrial aesthetic. But at the same time, downtown is advancing. The giants are coming! The real heroes of American Progress, after exhausting the fertile ground of the city center, like herds on mountain pastures, are looking for new land in which to sink their foundations. The street was opened up about two decades ago by the first high-rises right next to Market Street. Then came the Convention Center, the Museum of Modern Art, the stadium, and some other cultural facilities. And with these came the skyscrapers. Years ago, committees were formed to prevent the so-called Manhattanization of San Francisco. I don't know if they still exist. In any case, it seems that the battle had a two-pronged result: it discouraged the advance of downtown toward North Beach or Russian Hill; and, conversely, it caused an overflowing of high-rises of every type in the other direction, SoMa. By now, all cities tend to look alike. They are all copies of Manhattan. Why not San Francisco?

Van Ness | Aesthetically speaking, Van Ness Avenue is rather faceless; it is, however, an important street and a very practical one. In 1906, its great width allowed it to function as a firebreak in the enormous fire that destroyed half the city after the earthquake. All downtown San Francisco was razed to the ground right up to the edge of Van Ness. Beyond that point,

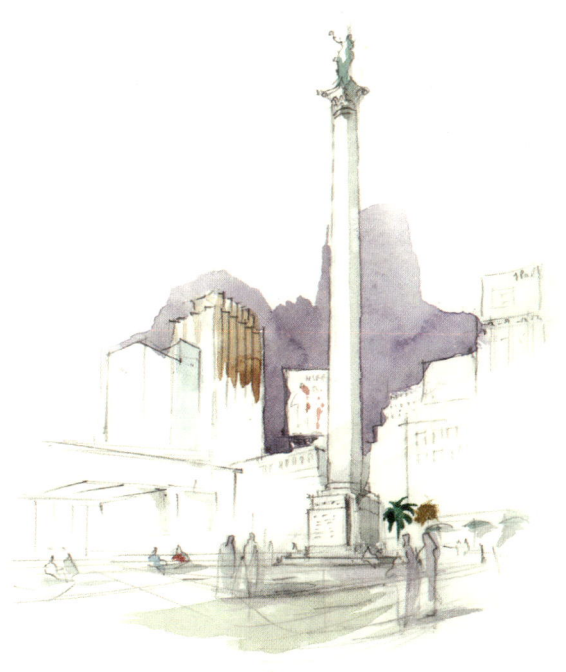

the city remained intact, and has maintained its unmistakable Victorian character until our day.

Today Van Ness is the fastest route for cutting across the city in a car, avoiding the countless stop signs and traffic lights of the parallel streets. It is a sort of urban freeway that takes on a majestic air only around the Beaux-Arts buildings of the Civic Center. There, it seems to toss a quick greeting to City Hall, then continue rapidly on its way.

Sounds | The window is open; a cable car clatters to its stop. A ding-dong of the bell, then it clatters off again. The hiss dies out at the bottom of the hill and melds with the horn of a ship passing on the bay. From the square comes a sound of bells, a sweet recorded carillon. In the street below, two men are talking; I don't recognize the language. A jet flies by, a barely perceptible roar in the distance. Other voices rise from the street, a distant murmur, other engines; the sound of the city enters the room on the wind.

Cable Cars | There is a building on the corner of Washington and Mason Streets that is the powerhouse for all the cable cars in the city. Like in a fairy-tale factory, four huge wheels inside this brick building turn with a deafening clang, pulling all the steel cables that run underneath the streets. The cable cars hook onto these cables to climb or descend the steepest hills.

On the street, the cable cannot be seen, but it can be heard wherever the rails run. Even if there are no cars in sight, you can always hear the constant rumble of the underground cable, this murmuring karst river, the hidden clangor of a nineteenth-century proto-industrial metropolis that seems never to stop moving. Under the metal gap two inches wide but many miles long, which together with the tracks mark so many streets of San Francisco with glittering steel, runs this wire ruled by a single huge motor. A motor housed in a little building that is the city's living, beating heart, creator of energy and movement.

A House | From outside, the little house, squeezed between the other Victorian buildings on the street, stands out: its entire front is made of shiny corrugated aluminum.

After a minimal zinc gate, a long, bare concrete staircase rises straight up to the entrance on the upper floor, since the ground floor is occupied by the garage. A metal door leads into the apartment: the two-story living room has a roof supported by white steel beams. Next to a black granite fireplace is a window without

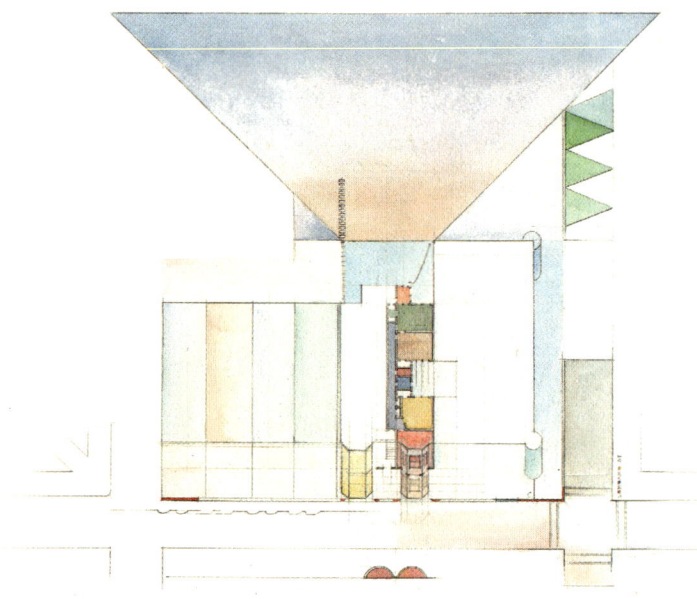

curtains or even fittings: only a glass square framing the Golden Gate Bridge in the distance. On the
left, beyond the glass door, is an outside deck of teak
planks and rubber and steel chaises longues. The living room floor is covered in light-colored resin, the
doors have flush retreating handles, the lights turn on
by the swipe of a fingertip across the switch. On the

walls are abstract paintings and some black-and-white photos of landscapes. Art and design books, an Eames table, different chairs, a Bertoia, one by Breuer.

I open the window and go out on the deck. A cool evening breeze is blowing. I look around: the pointed roofs of the houses, the high terraces, the silver light of sunset, the first lighted windows. I look again at the Golden Gate Bridge far away. The fog is rolling in, soon the bridge will disappear. I feel a shiver, then Coltrane's sax wafts out of the room. Chilly, I go back in; a fire has just been lit in the fireplace.

Two Bridges | The Golden Gate Bridge is all one bridge, a great gate for ships, a single wide road open to the sky. The Bay Bridge, on the contrary, is really three or four bridges with an island in the middle, two over-lapping freeways, a series of multiple portals for ships.

The Golden Gate Bridge is a transgressive red, the work of artists, its pylons elegantly pierced by Art Deco square openings. The Bay Bridge is a mass of silver-gray steel, no frills, with X-shaped pylons, perhaps overcalculated by superpractical engineers.

The Golden Gate Bridge is courageous, with its record leap across the water, its braving the ocean winds. The Bay Bridge is solid, static, safe, maybe even a little boring.

Everyone loves the Golden Gate Bridge. Many people love the Bay Bridge.

Old Berkeley | I am in the yard of a suburban house in Berkeley, built around the 1920s. The lawn, on a slight slope, is dominated by three very tall redwood trees; someone told me that they are at least three hundred years old. Each one is made up of two or three reddish trunks that rise from the ground like arrows shot toward the sky. The exterior of the house is covered with shingles, reddish like the trunks of the redwoods; the building has a nineteenth-century look, with bay windows, flower boxes, porch, and pitched roofs punctuated by brick chimneys. I am reminded of Maybeck, the Green brothers, the Bay Region style, the times gone by when architects wore starched collars and bow ties.

The Arts and Crafts style is even more evident inside the house. Wainscots and molding of dark wood dominate the smooth white walls. Coffered ceilings, fireplaces, staircases with good sturdy railings, also of dark oak. And clerestories, large rooms, smaller hallways and landings, lots of cupboards for storage, cabinets, shelves, and hardwood floors everywhere, laid in a herringbone pattern. This house is the perfect image of old Berkeley, a city that grew up around the turn of the twentieth century. Reinforcing this atmosphere are glimpses through the trees of the white roofs of the grand Claremont Hotel a few blocks away.

Who knows why the Claremont, a monument to the fabulous local past, was painted white? Maybe so it would stand out more visibly, as though this fantastic castle in the Shingle style did not stand out enough already. Here where I am is the intimate, private house; a short distance away is the hotel, a pure white mountain, snow-topped, with public terraces, pools, sun deck, porte-cochere, lobbies, bar, and restaurants.

The Claremont Hotel is an immense miniature of a city. As in a crystal or an organic form, every architectural element seems to derive by parthenogenesis from other similar forms: shed roofs set into other shed roofs, dormer windows above other dormer windows, towers next to towers, domes and smaller domes, and finally a tall gable with an enormous American flag. This miniature city emerges in the midst of tall palm trees, weeping eucalyptuses, oaks, and crimson maples.

White and joyous: the Claremont Hotel does not transmit a sense of awe or magniloquence. It is monumental but also cozy; its volume, even though towering, is not threatening precisely because it is broken up into a countless number of smaller volumes. It is an open, calm, sunny building—different in any case from its contemporary Grand Hotels in Europe, its cousins across the sea: it is something more rustic, similar to, if anything, a lodge in a national park. A symbol of a bygone era, it is the icon of the America that once was.

Distances | From the house in Berkeley to the freeway, an urban stretch: streets, trees, houses, five minutes, ten with traffic. Average speed 30 miles per hour.

From the freeway entrance to the Bay Bridge, hills, views, roller-coaster road, five minutes, ten with traffic. Average speed 60 miles per hour.

From the Bay Bridge to the Golden Gate Bridge, urban stretch: streets, intersections, stop signs, traffic lights, houses, ten minutes, twenty with traffic. Average speed 20 miles per hour.

From the Golden Gate Bridge to Tiburon, the bridge, the ocean, the bay, the San Francisco skyline, seven minutes, fifteen with traffic. Average speed 60 miles per hour.

From Tiburon to the Richmond Bridge, valleys, dips, mountains, the horizon, eight minutes, twenty with traffic. Average speed 60 miles per hour.

From Richmond Bridge to Berkeley, driving over the water, profiles of hills, other horizons, seven minutes, fifteen with traffic. Average speed 60 miles per hour.

The circumnavigation of the bay is complete. A trip through three different territories (East Bay, San Francisco, Marin County), linked with each other by three bridges. Two urban stretches, all the others outside the

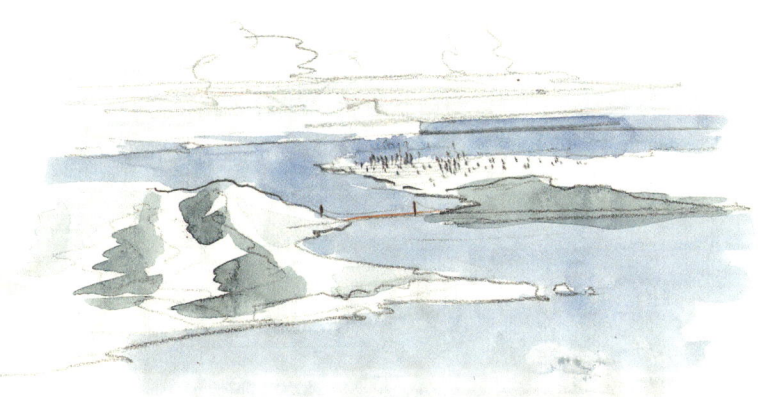

city, forty-three minutes in all, an hour and a half with traffic.

The experience of a territory is transmitted by its distances, by the time it takes to reach its different places; it is the whole of the sensations felt in movement, in the variations in altitude, in the time it takes for a landscape to change, in speed in relation to views, in the different perception of the things running past or the horizons that slip by in the distance.

Surroundings | Berkeley: a white bell tower. Oakland: high-rises and freeways. Sausalito, Belvedere, and Tiburon: Portofinos by the bay. Daly City: San Francisco's backyard. San José: invisible from here.

Foghorn | Maybe I was already awake or maybe it was in a dream that I heard the ship's horn. A repeated, slow cry, almost the lament of a desperate animal, a dark, dense, deep, dragged-out sound. Then silence. Then the cry once again. It is an immense ship crossing through the fog on the bay. A giant that goes its way unseen, after the ocean, heading for port.

107